SONGBOOK OF THE DEAD

HALLOWEEN MUSIC FOR THE PIANO

MUSIC BY DRAKE DESCANT
ART BY DUSTIN STELZER

TABLE OF CONTENTS

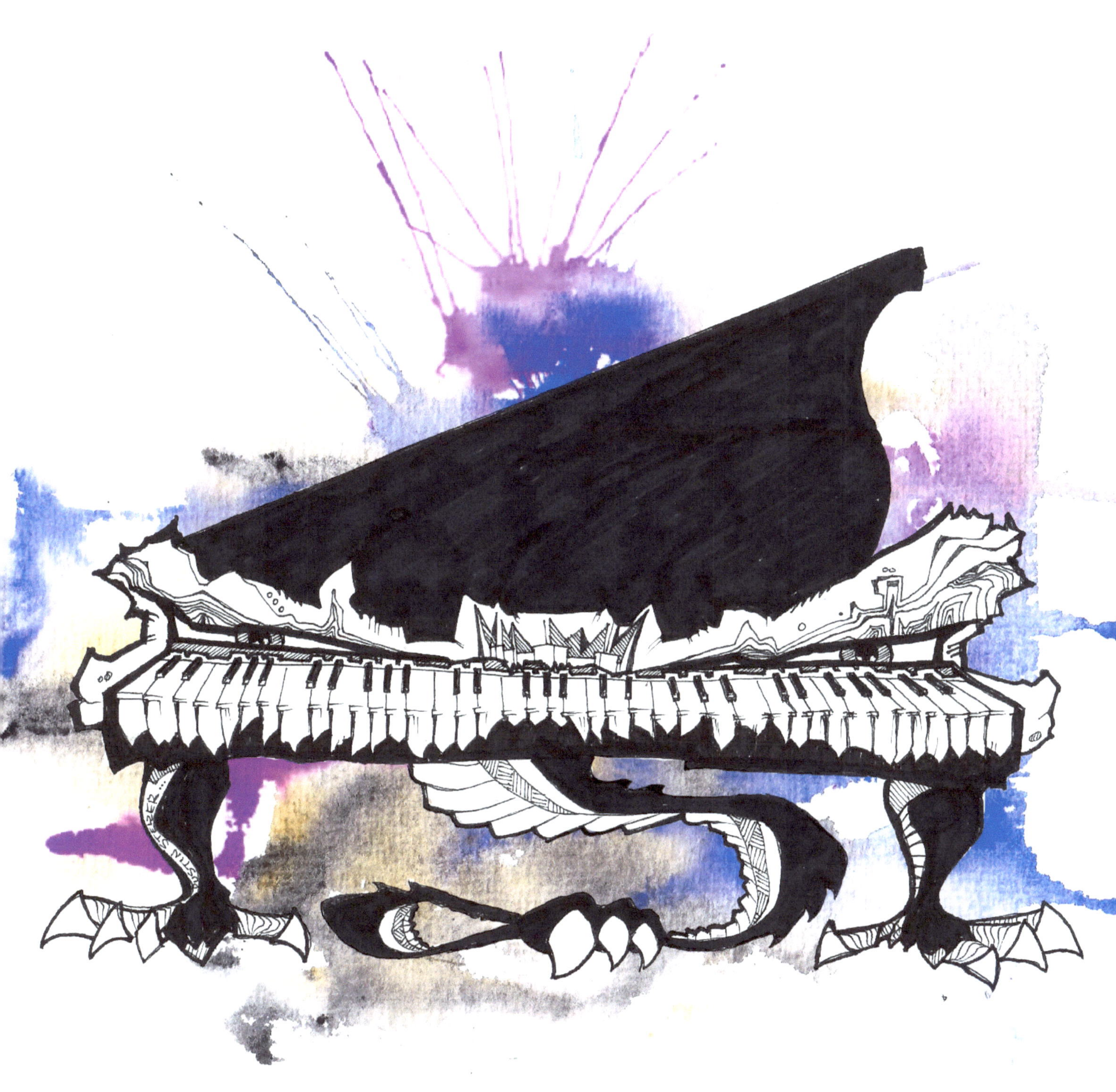

SEND US AN EMAIL AT THESONGBOOKOFTHEDEAD@GMAIL.COM

FOR FREE AUDIO FILES OF ALL THESE SONGS

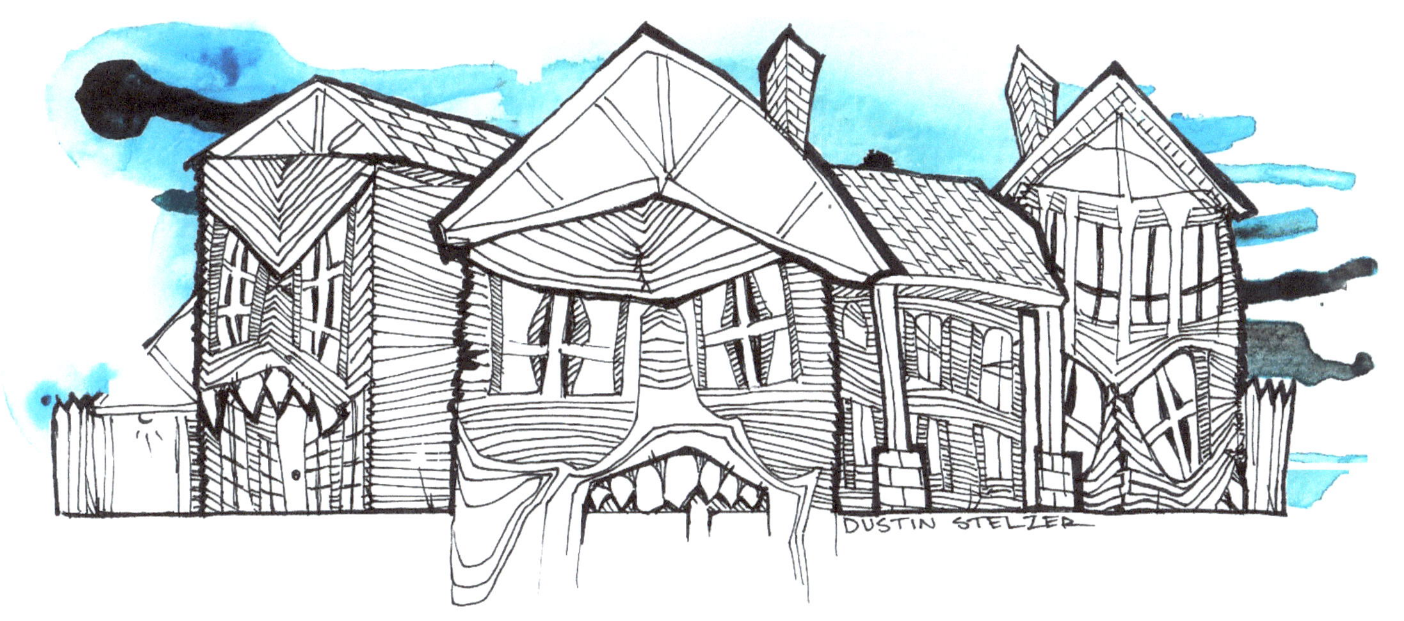

AROUND THE HAUNTED MANSION

DRAKE DESCANT

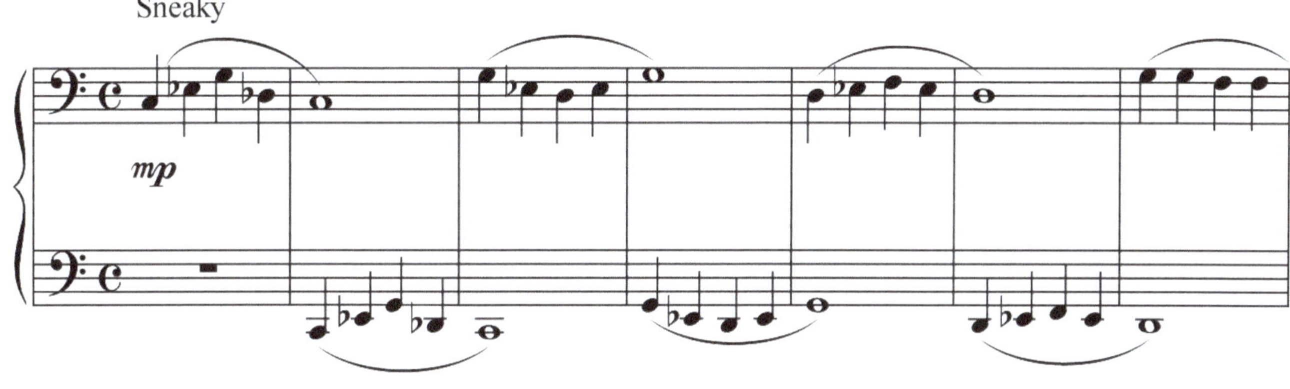

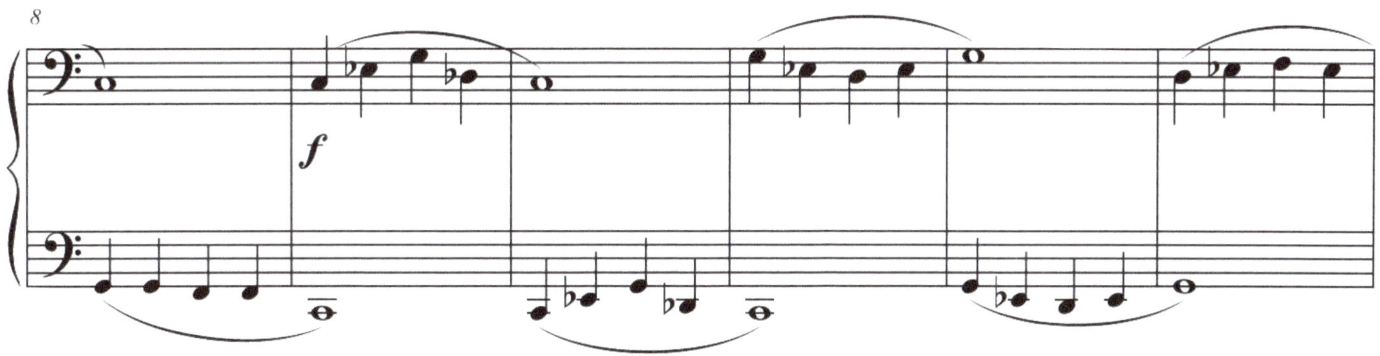

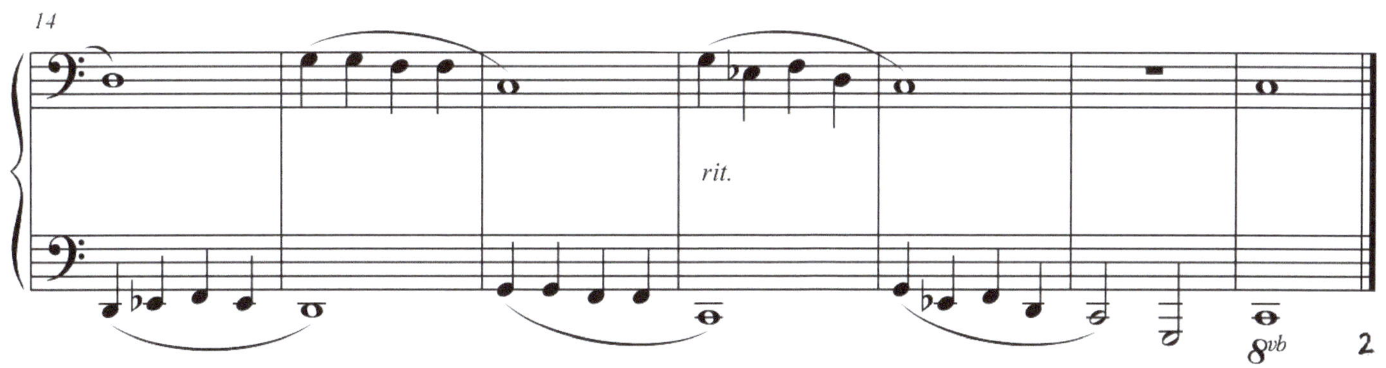

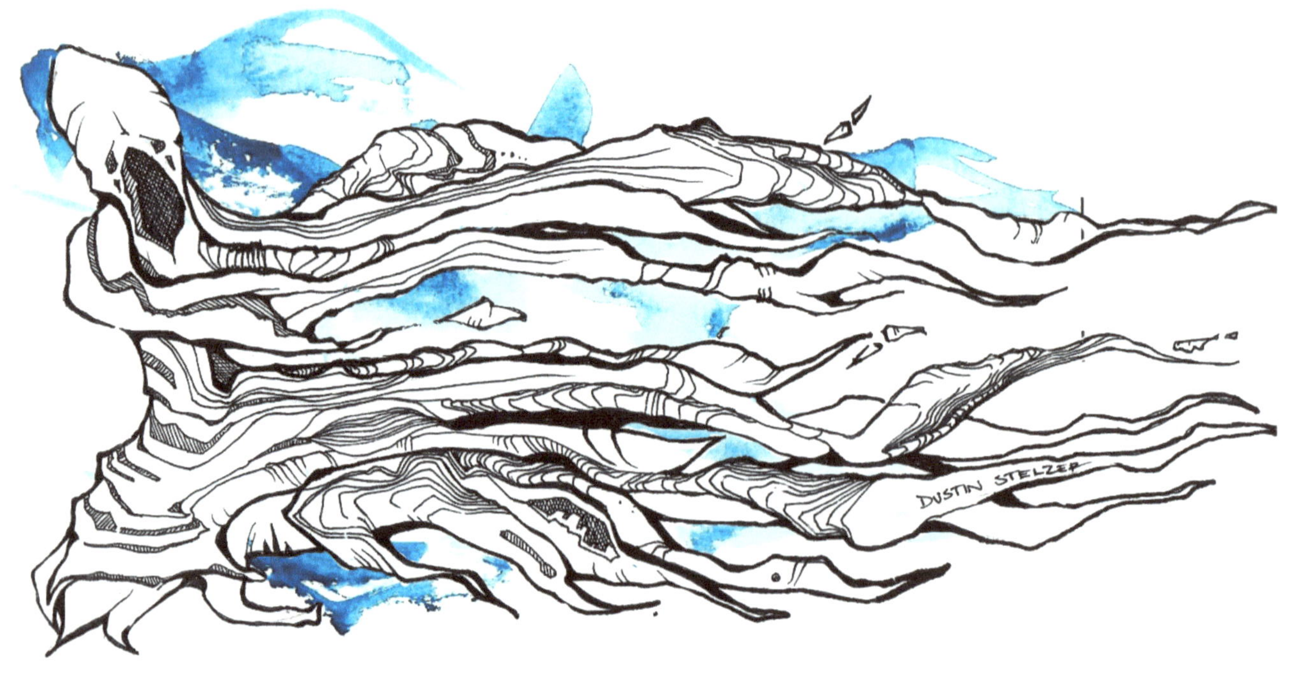

LONELY GHOST WALTZ

DRAKE DESCANT

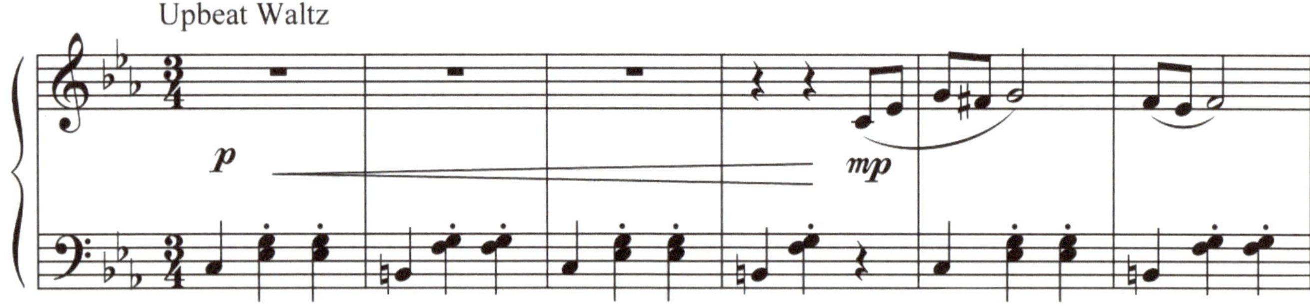

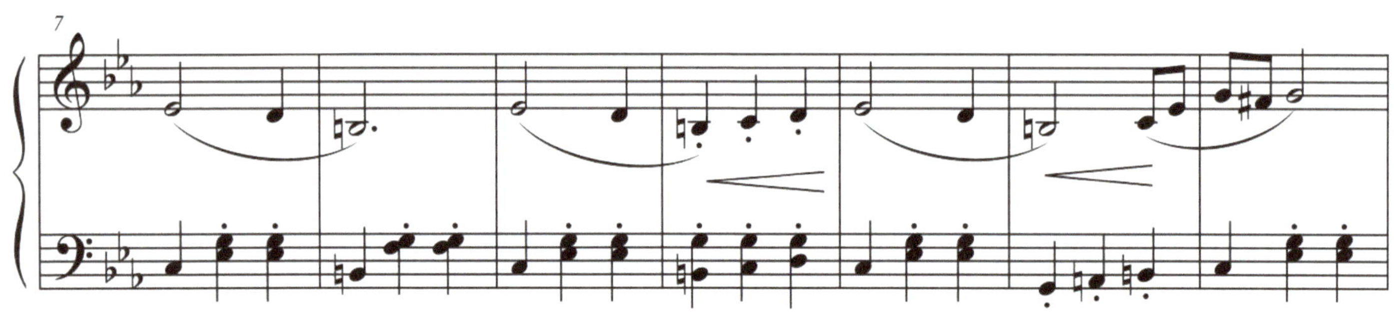

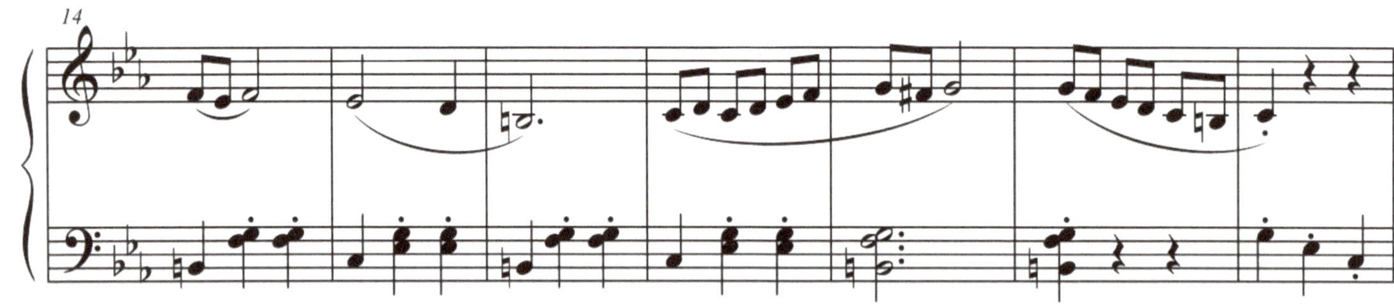

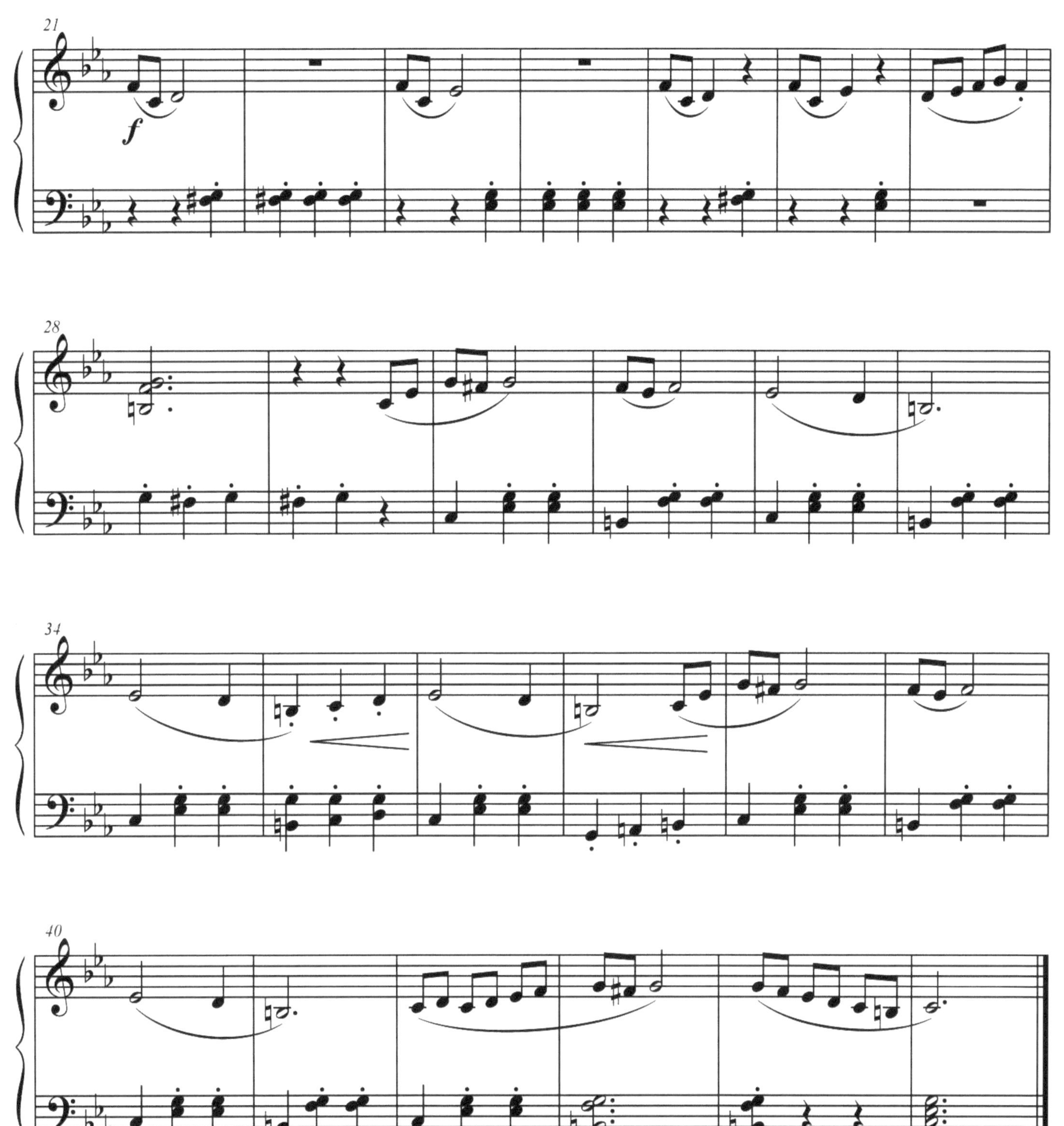
21
f
28
34
40

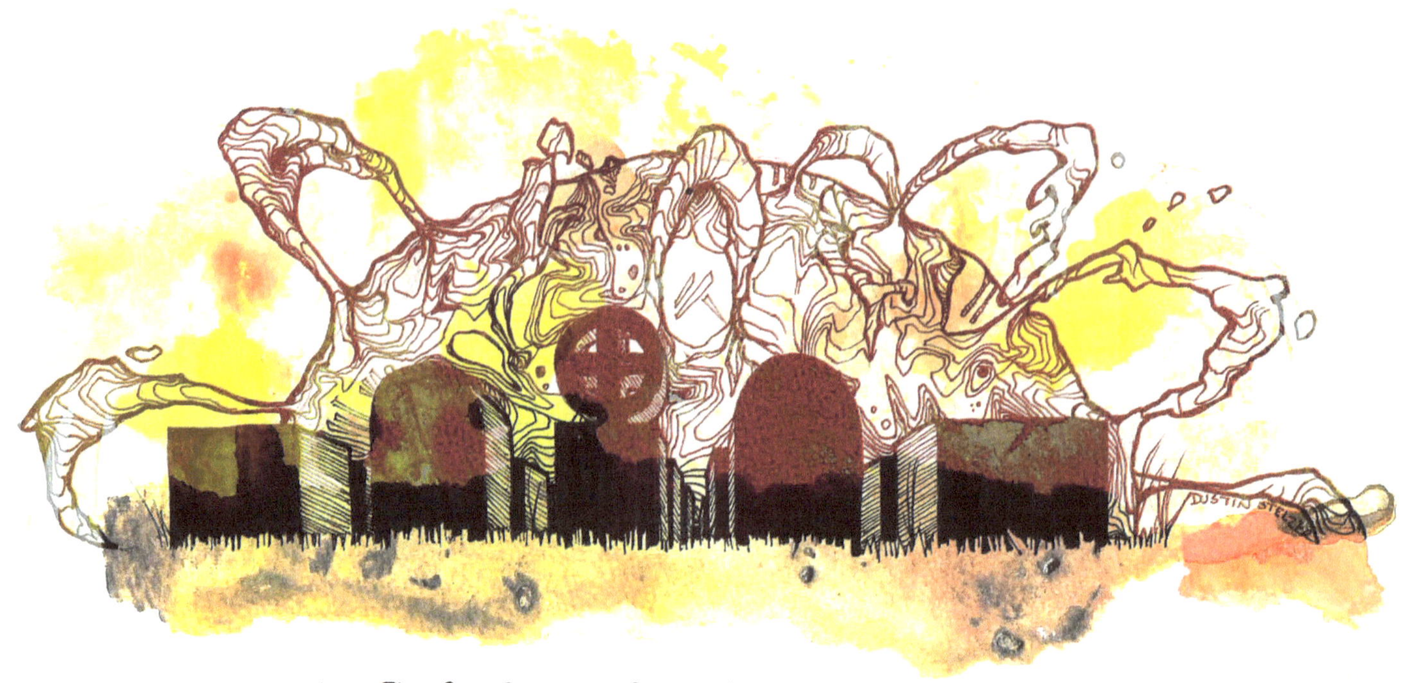

CEMETERY SUNSET

DRAKE DESCANT

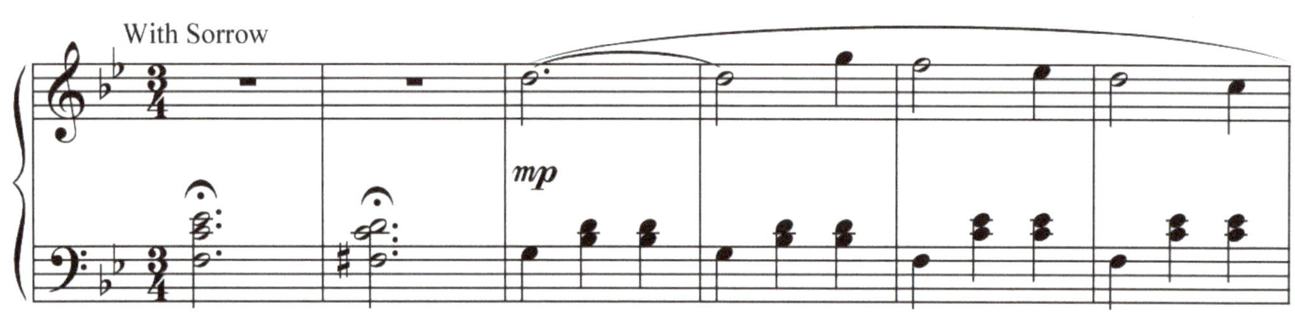

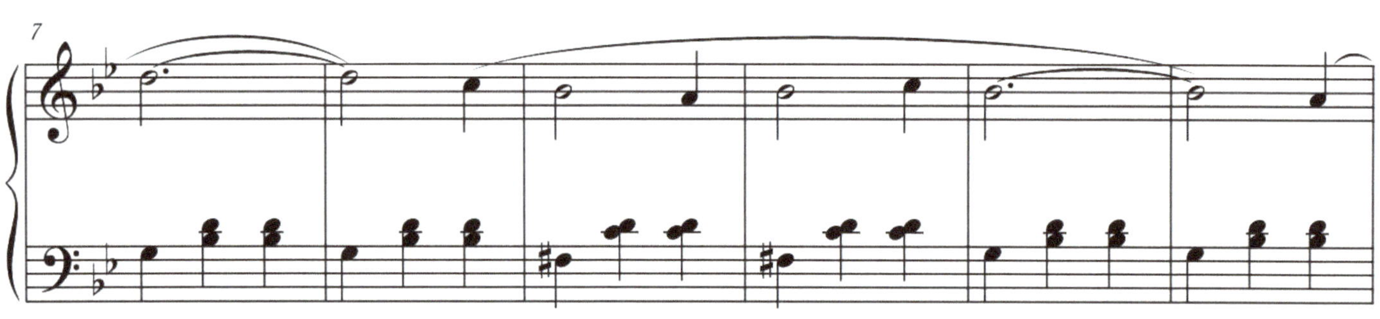

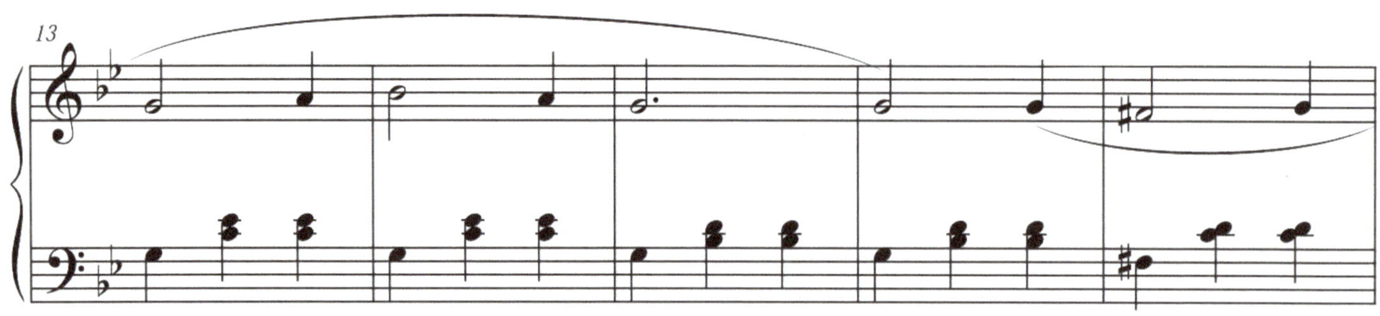

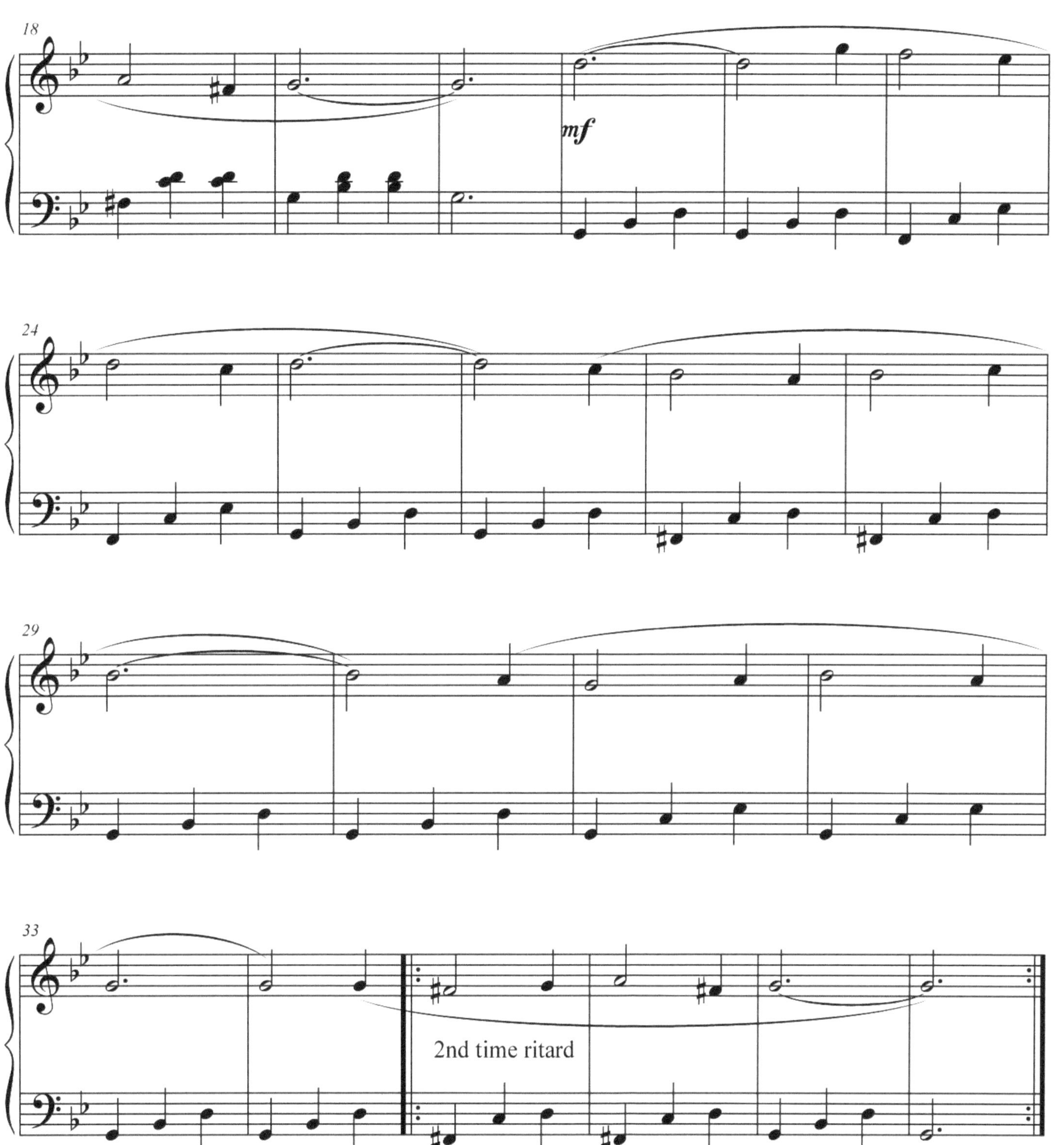
18
mf
24
29
33
2nd time ritard

THE ZOMBIE MARCH

DRAKE DESCANT

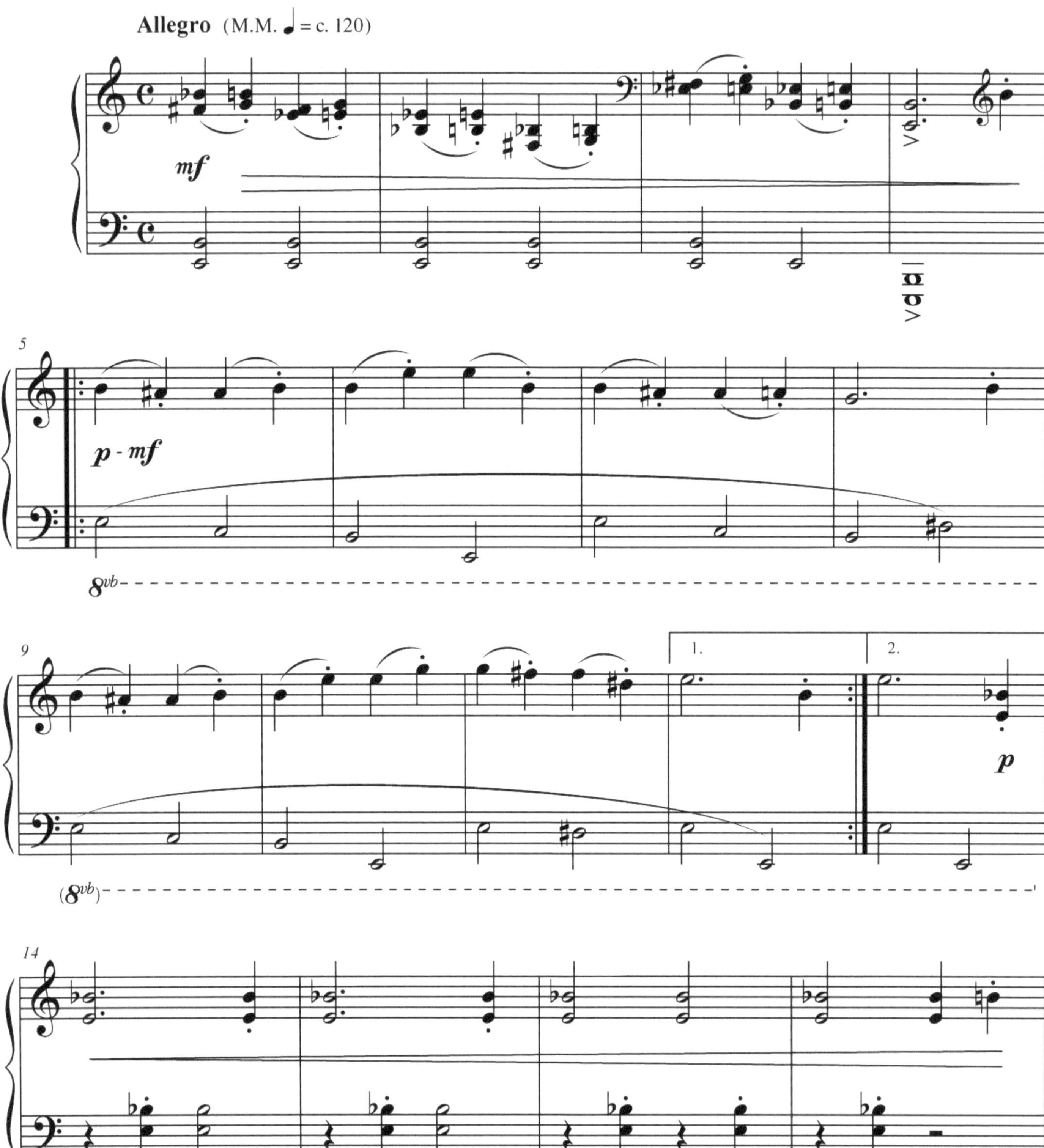

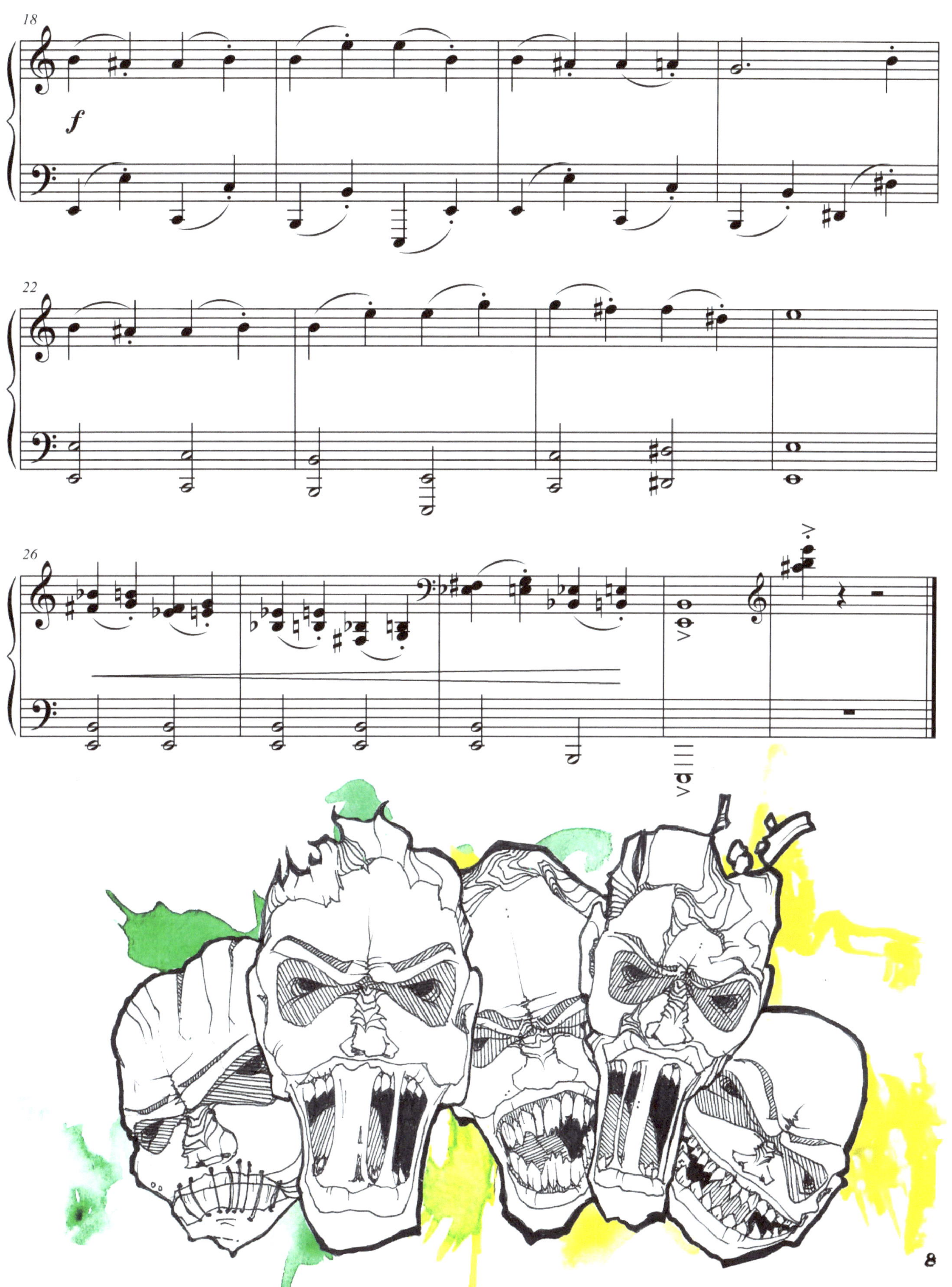
18
f
22
26

HALLOWEEN NIGHTMARE

DRAKE DESCANT

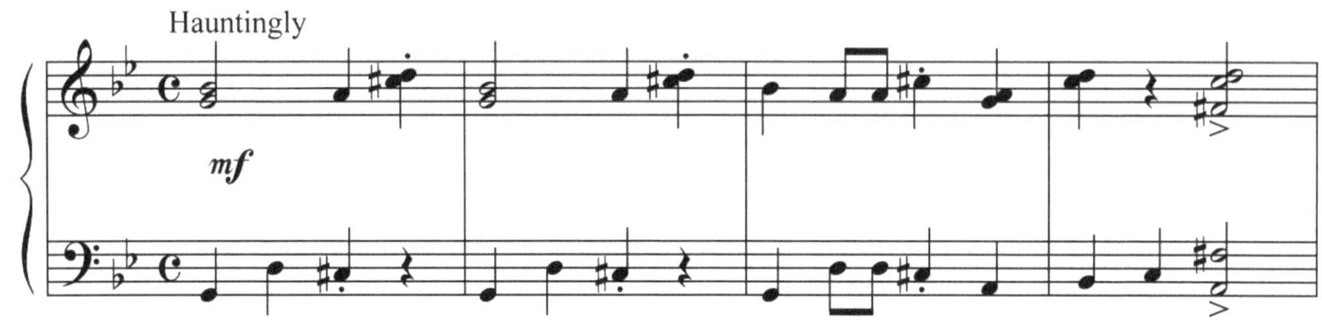

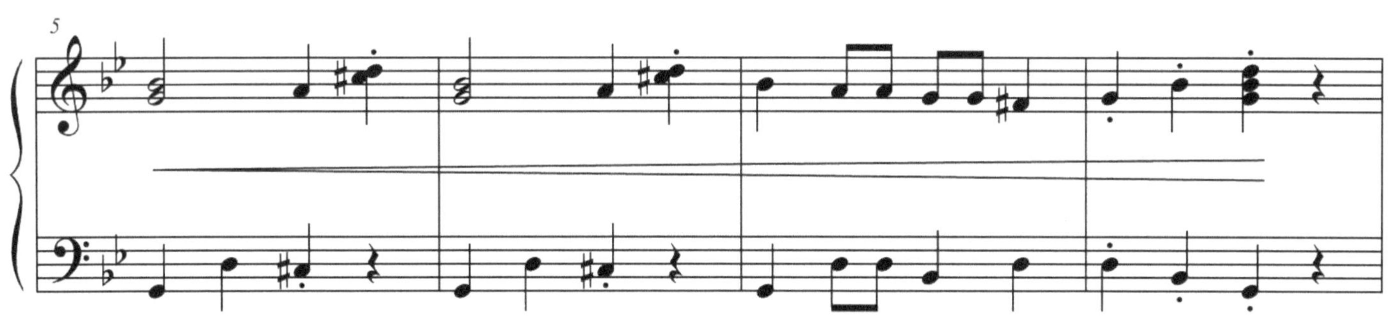

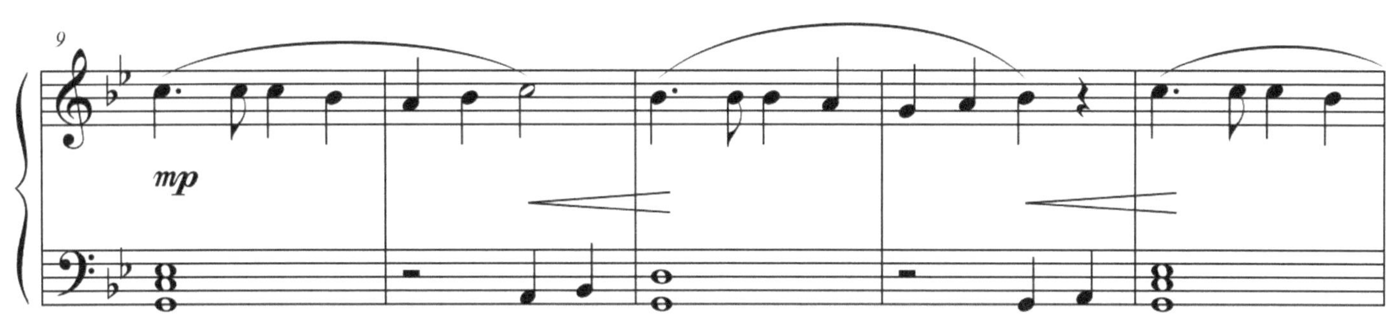

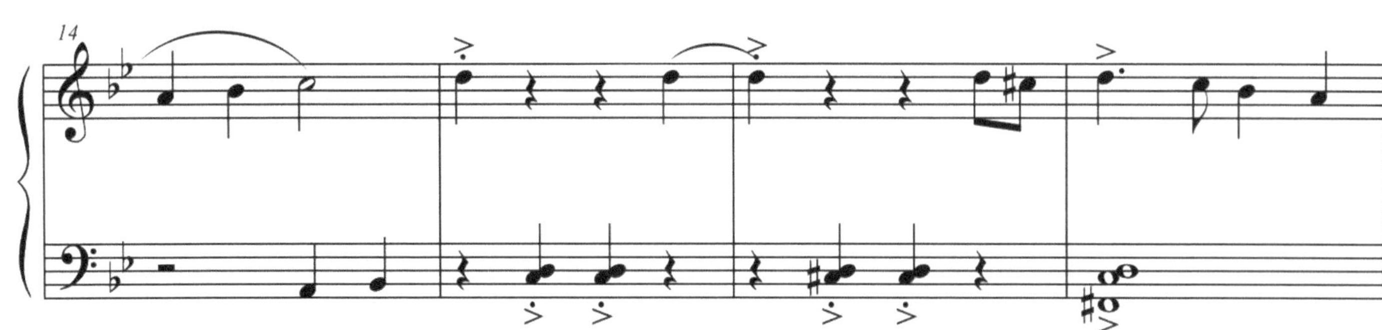

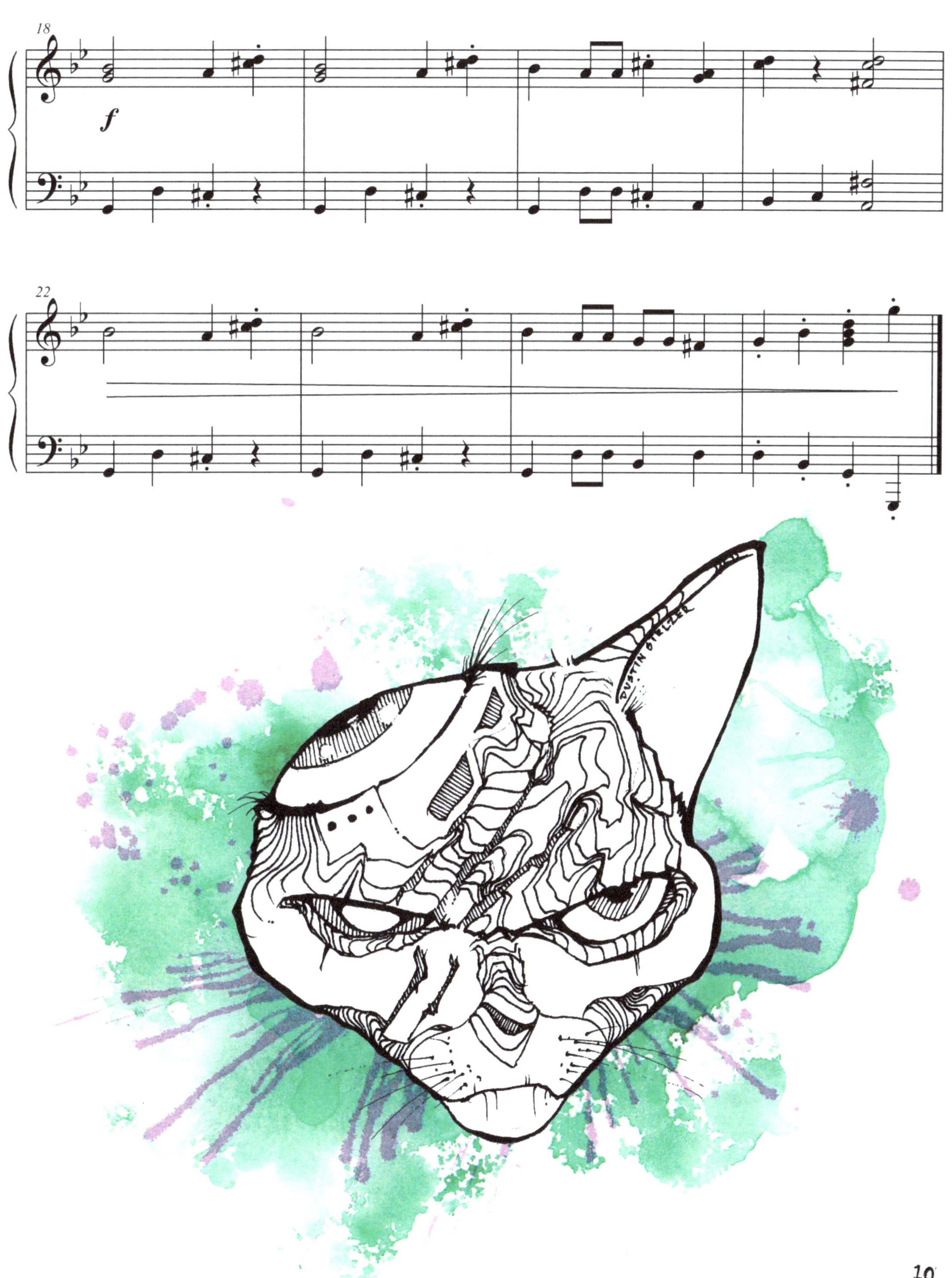
18
f
22

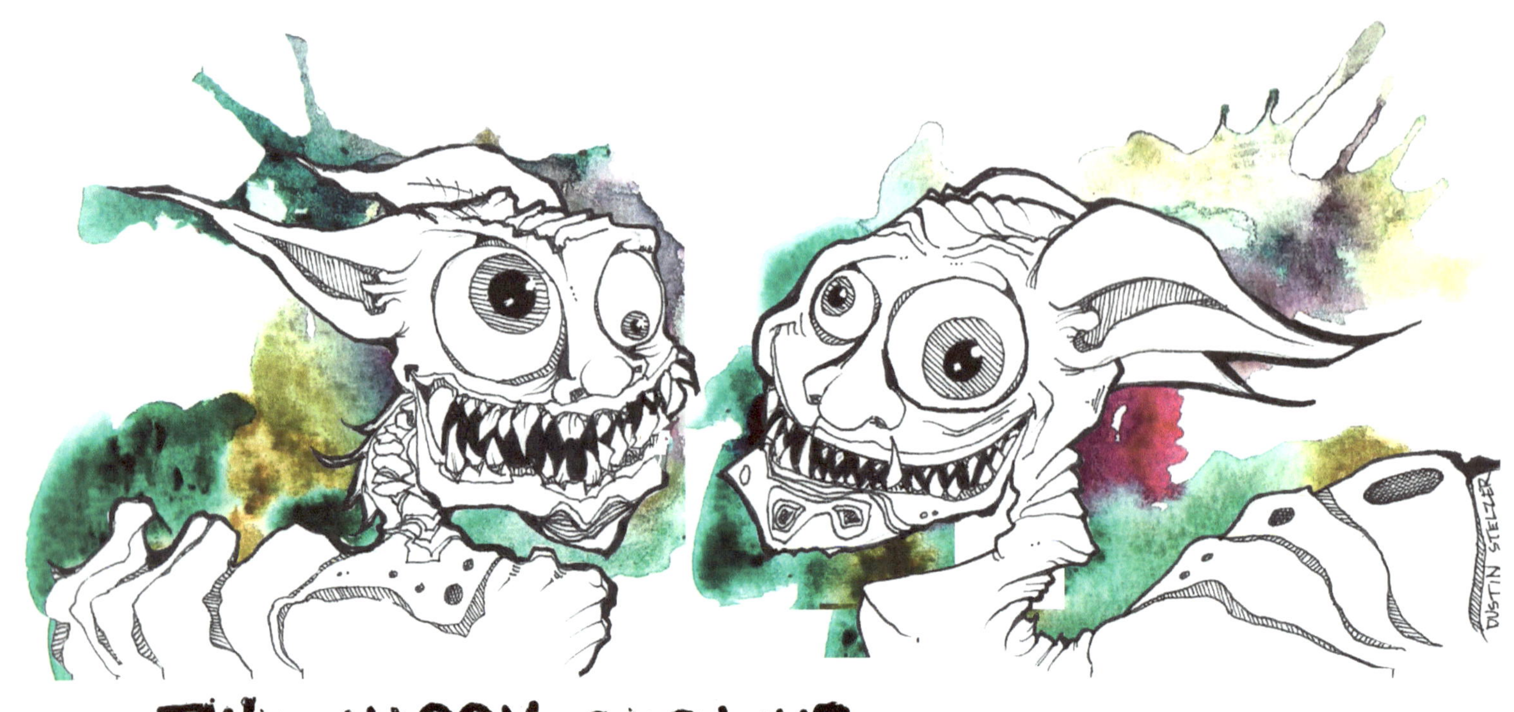

DRAKE DESCANT

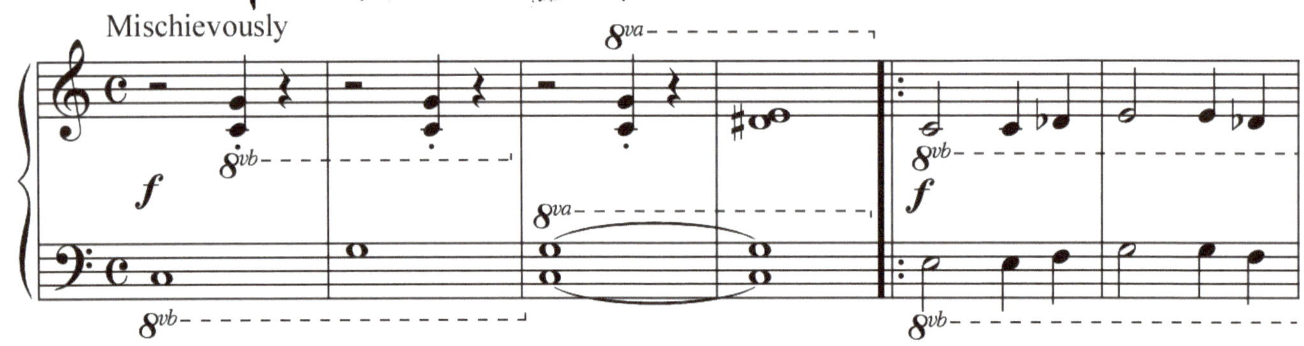

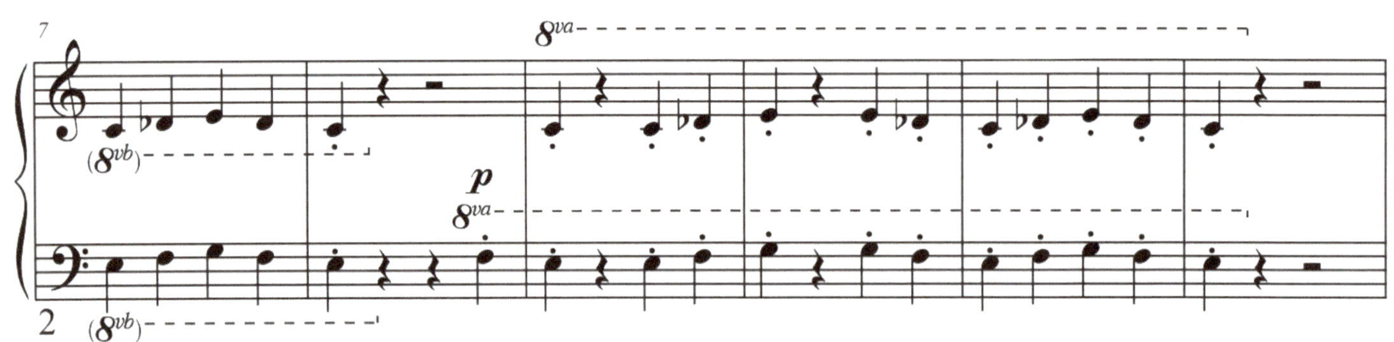

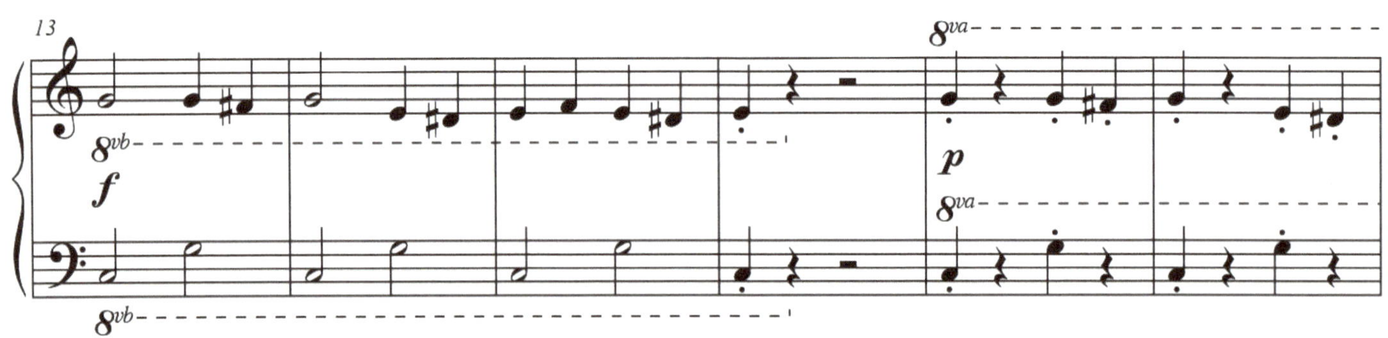

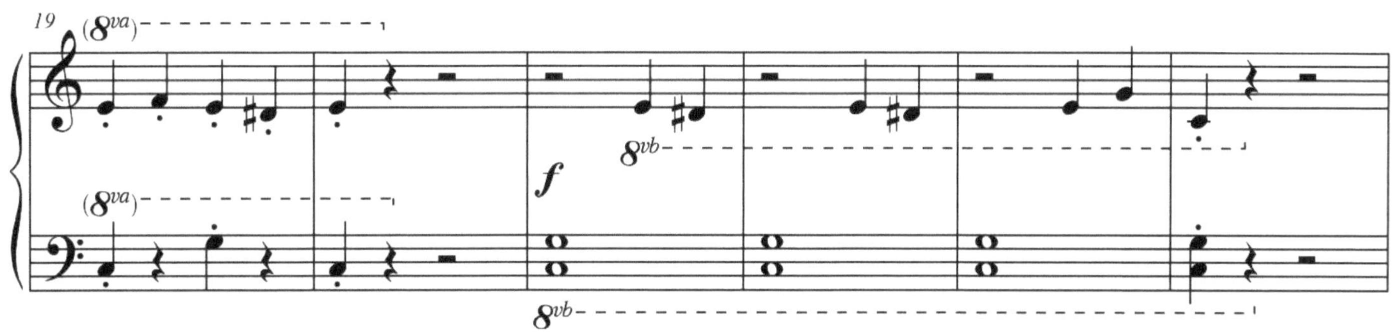
19
(8va)
f
8vb

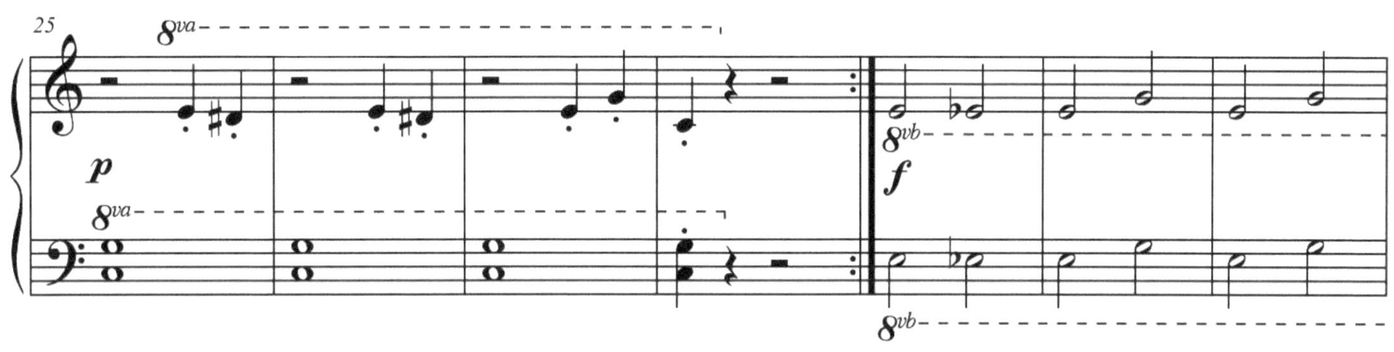
25
8va
p
8vb
f

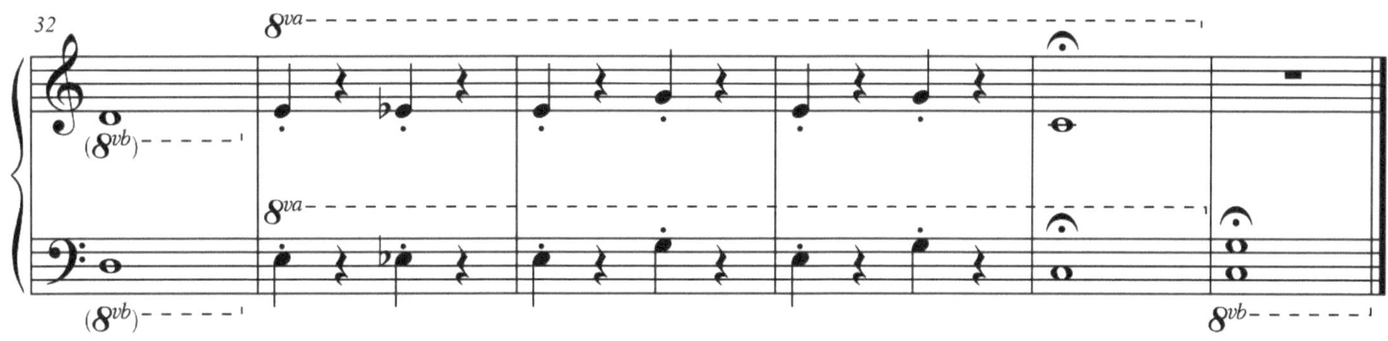
32
8va
(8vb)
8vb

BROKEN TOY

DRAKE DESCANT

With Feeling

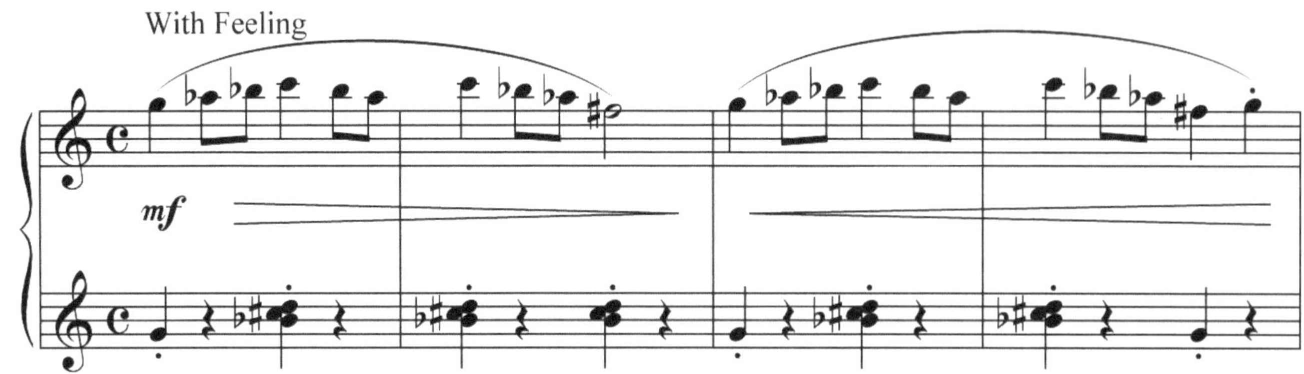

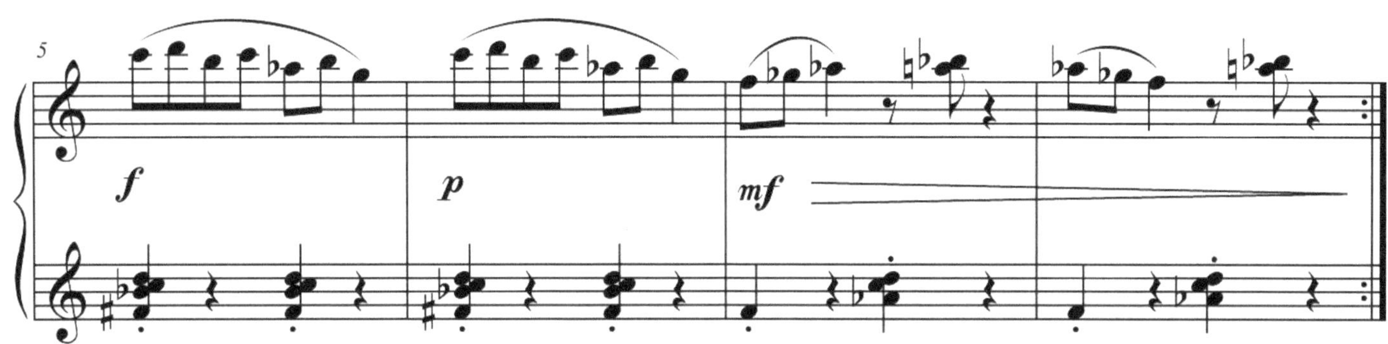

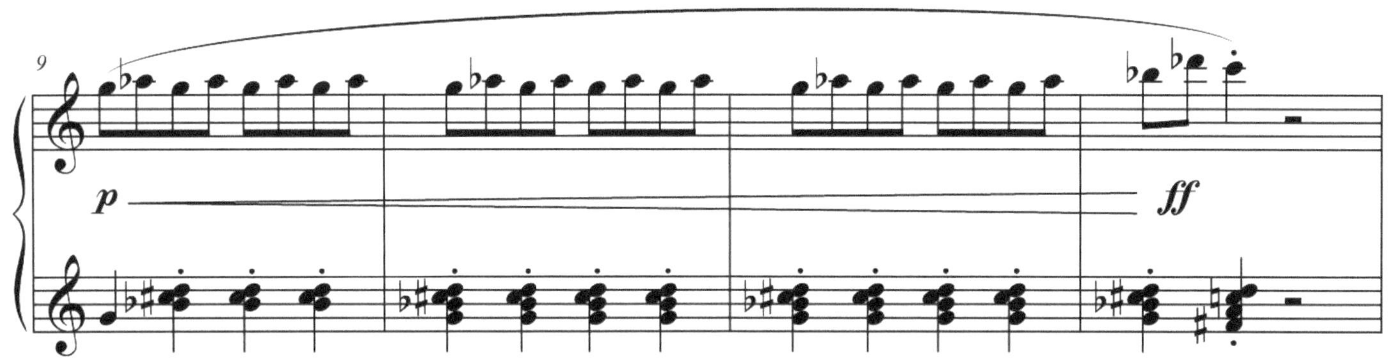

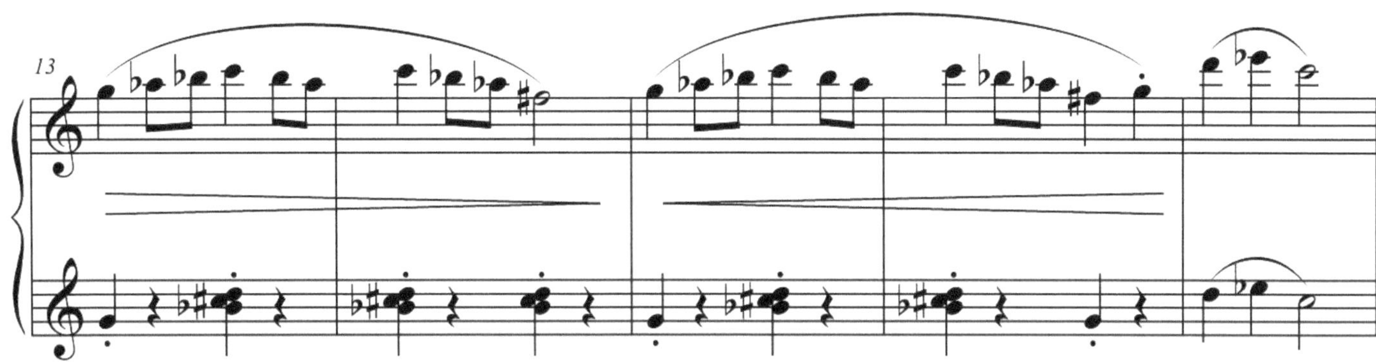

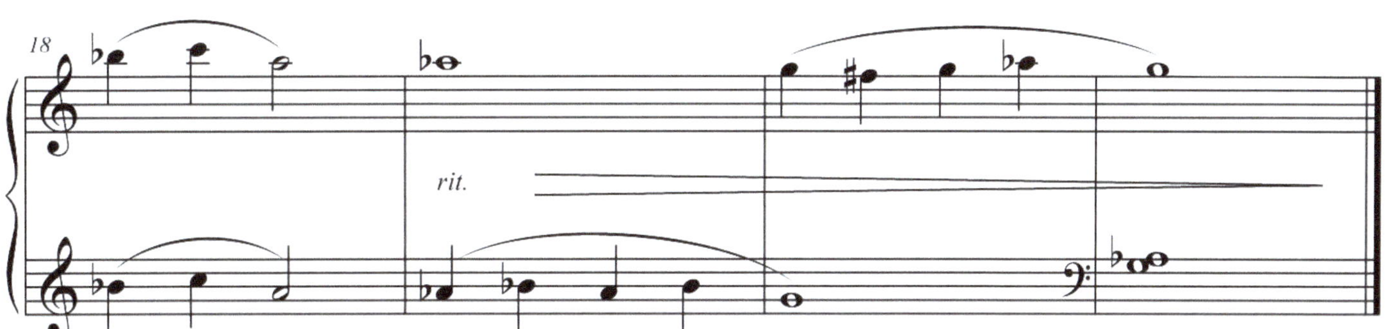
18
rit.

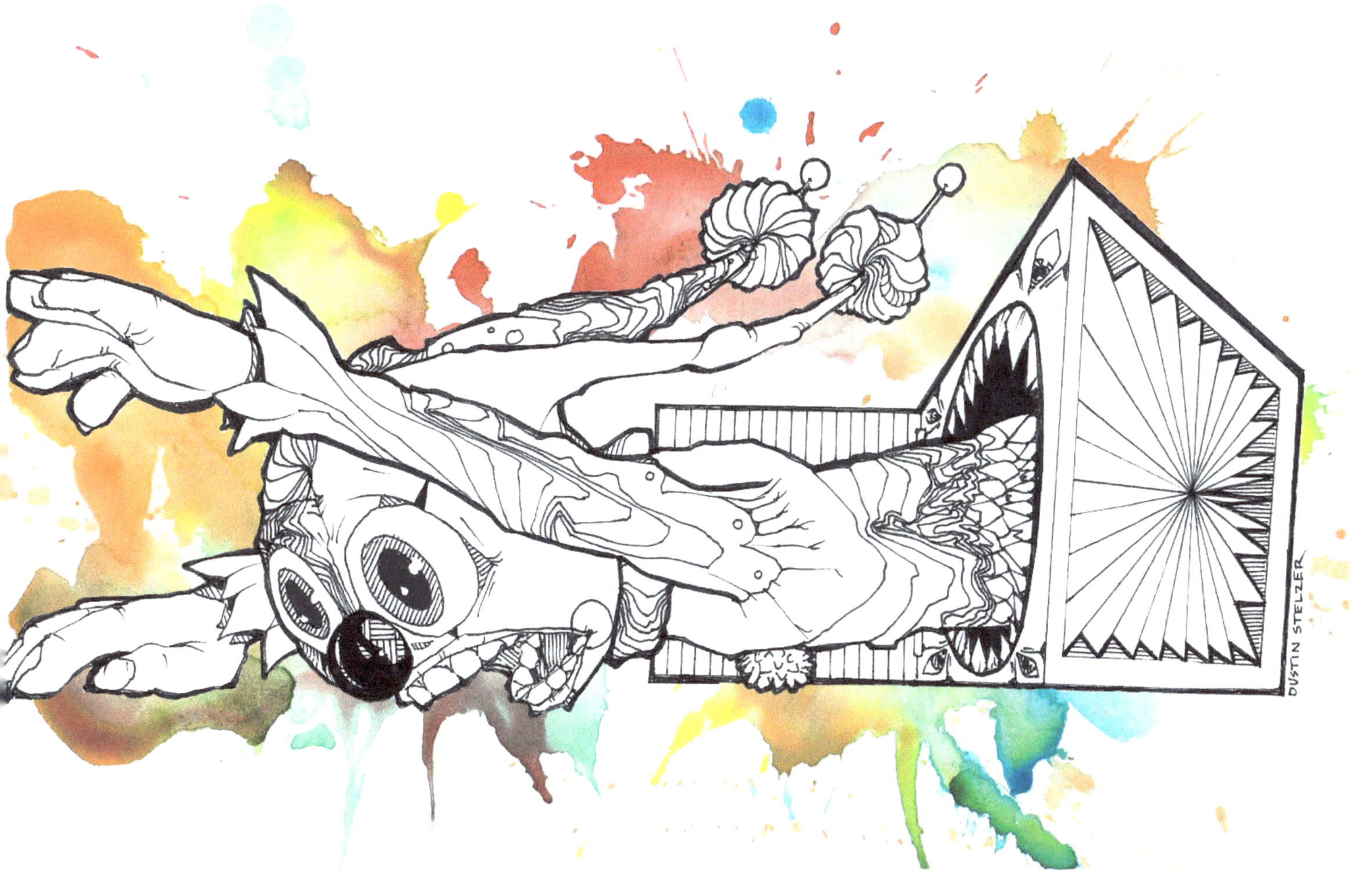

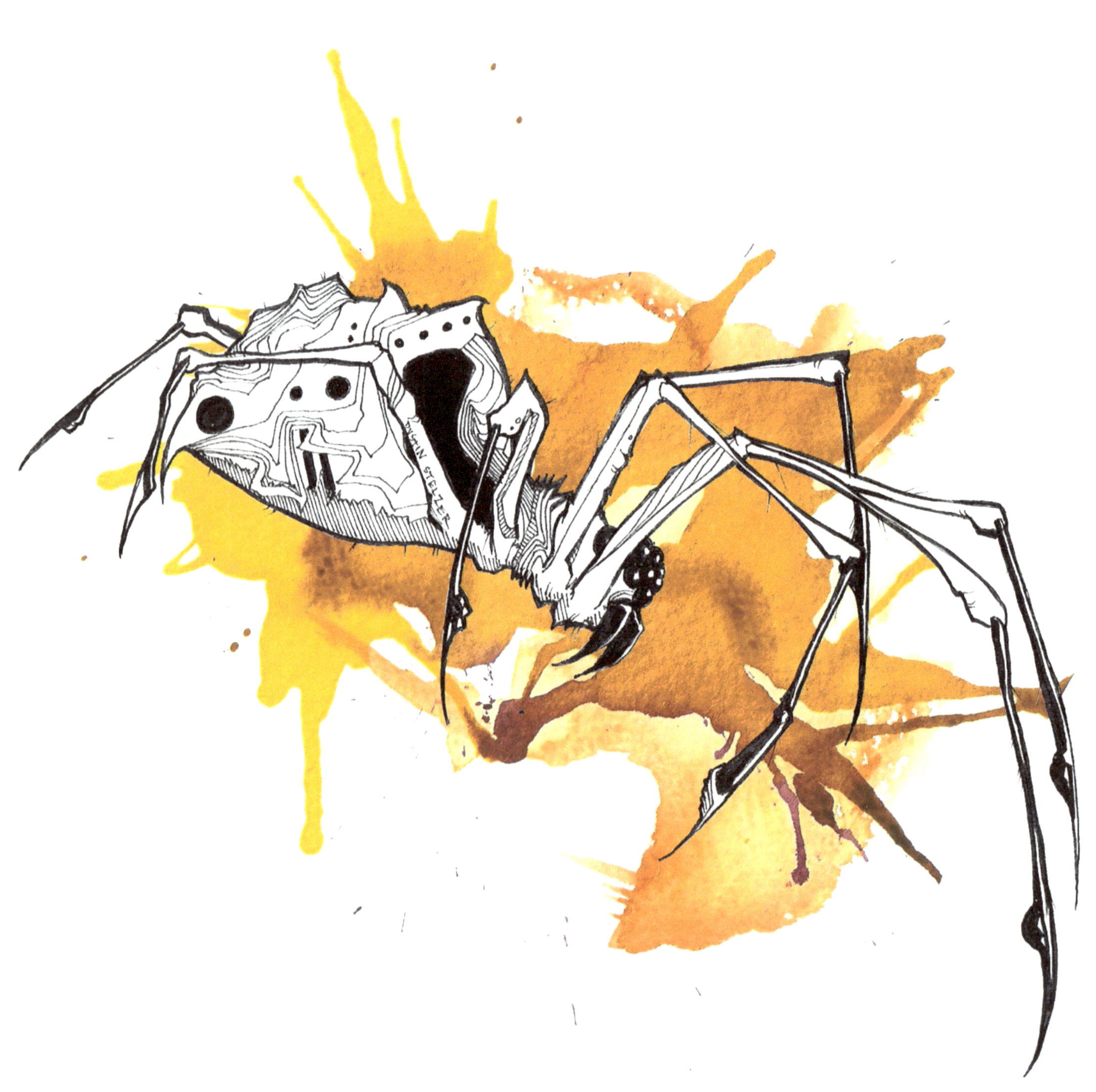
DUSTIN STELZER

THE LURKING SPIDER

DRAKE DESCANT

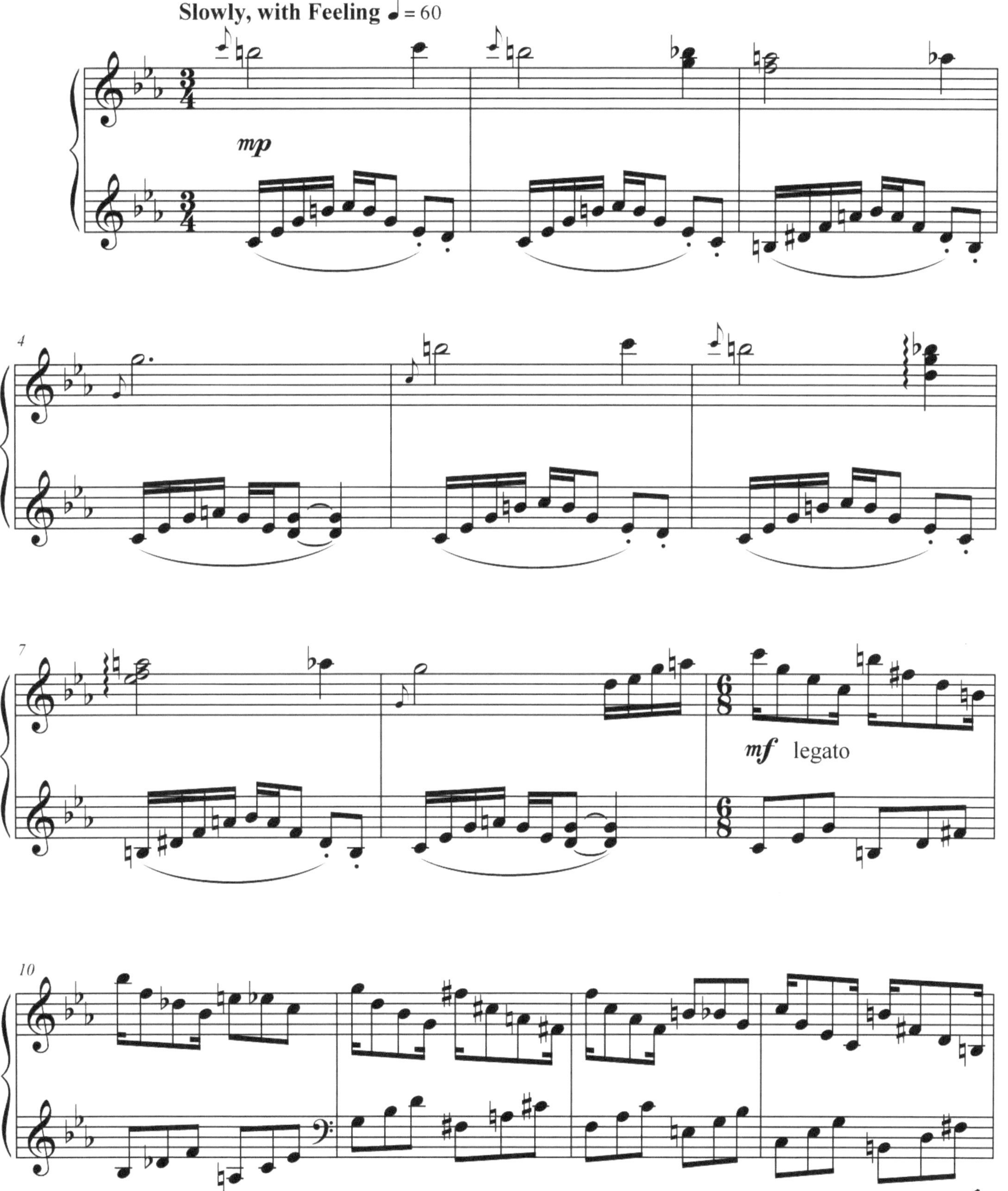

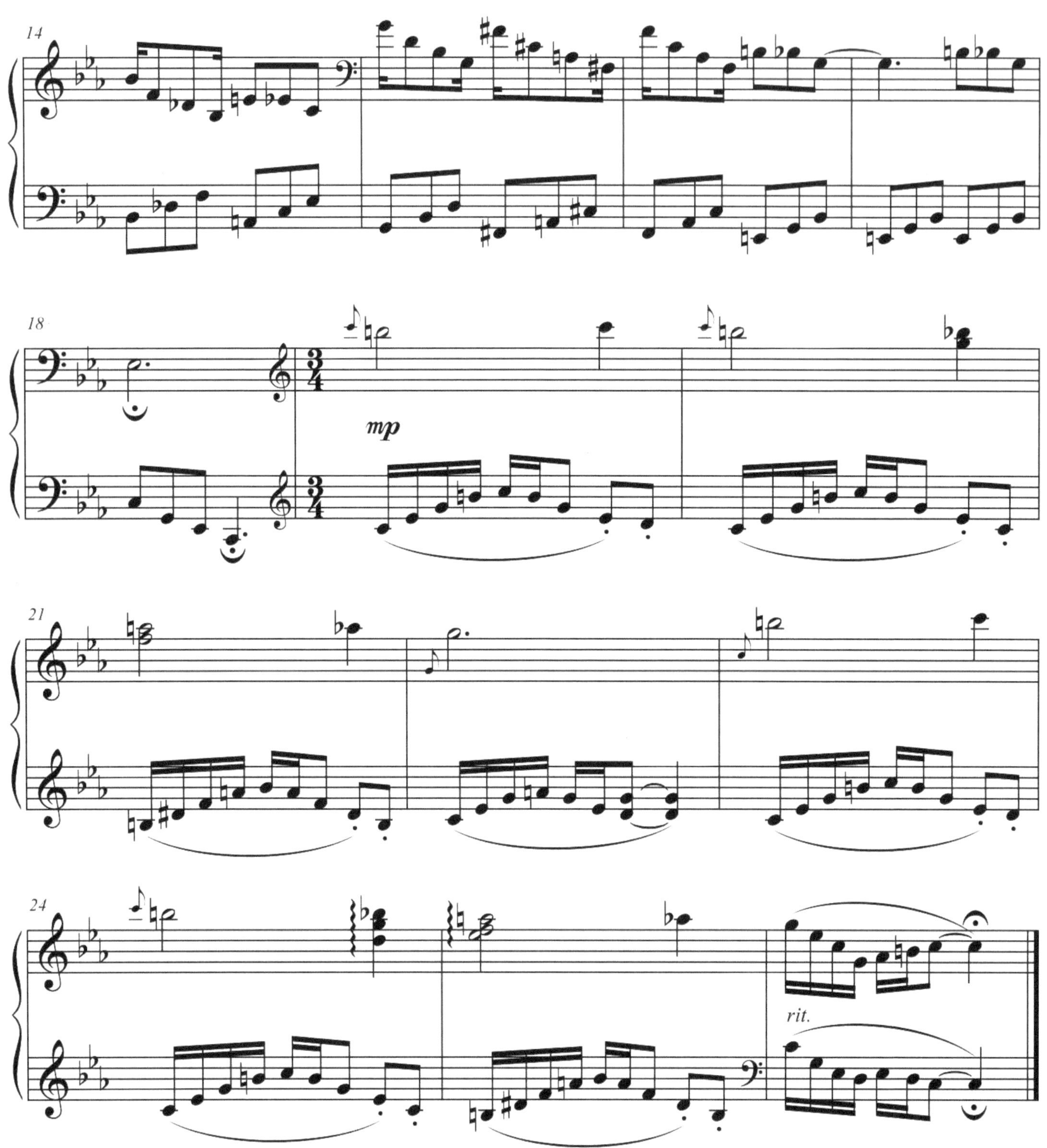
14
18
mp
21
24
rit.

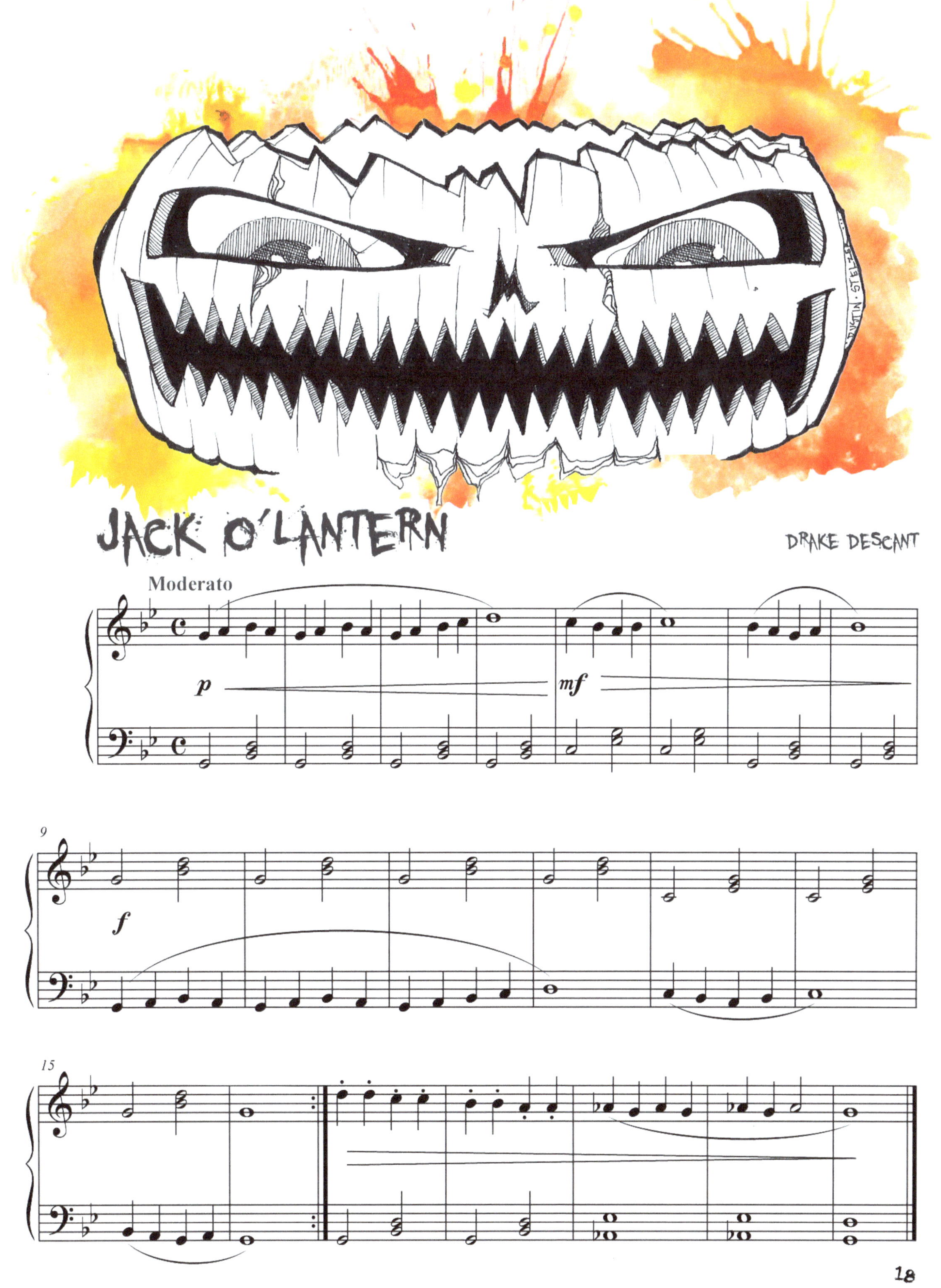
JACK O'LANTERN
DRAKE DESCANT
Moderato
p
mf
9
f
15

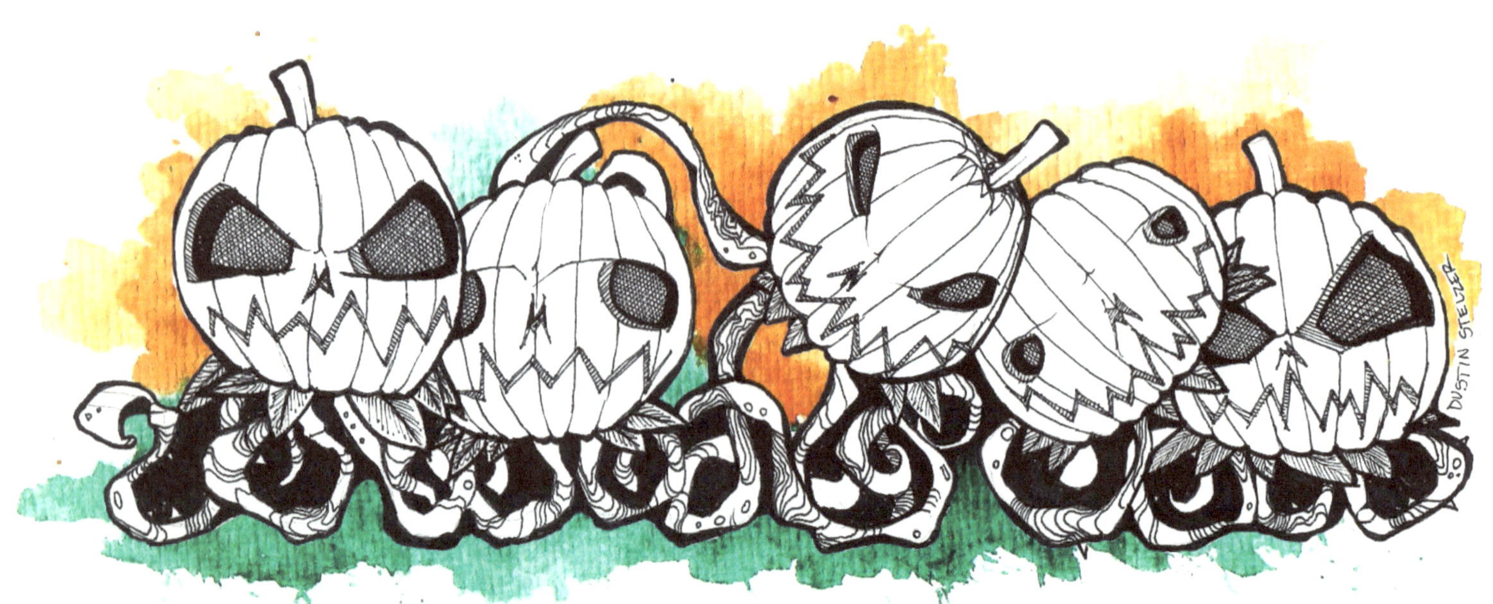

THE PUMPKIN PATCH DANCE

DRAKE DESCANT

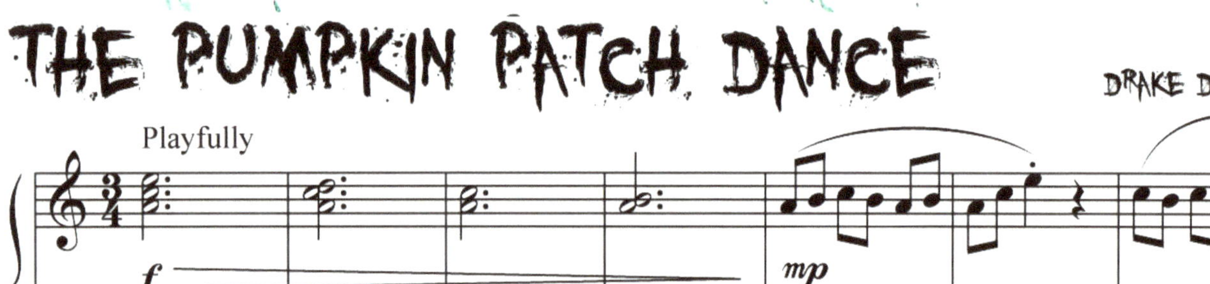

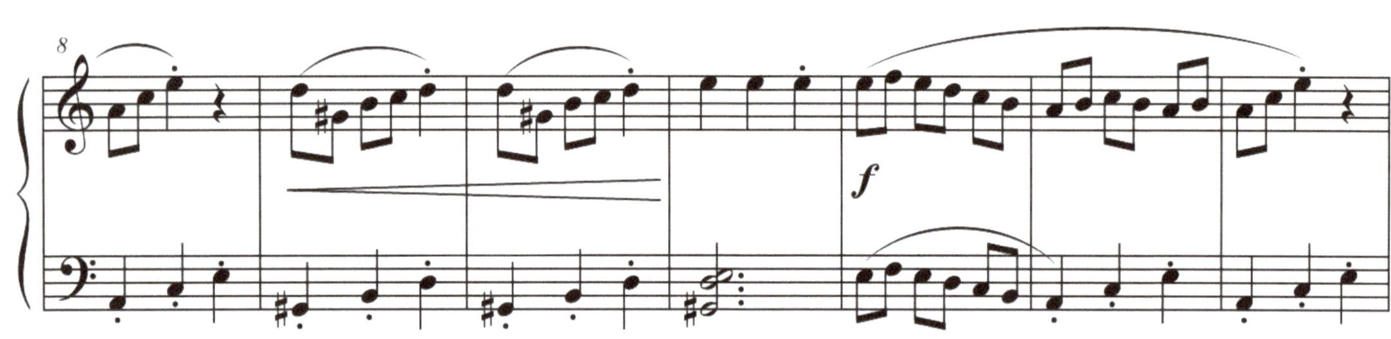

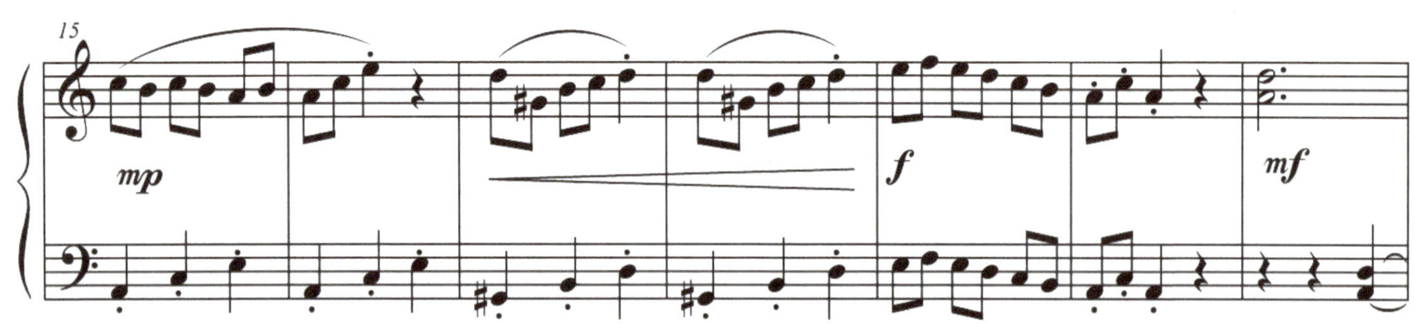

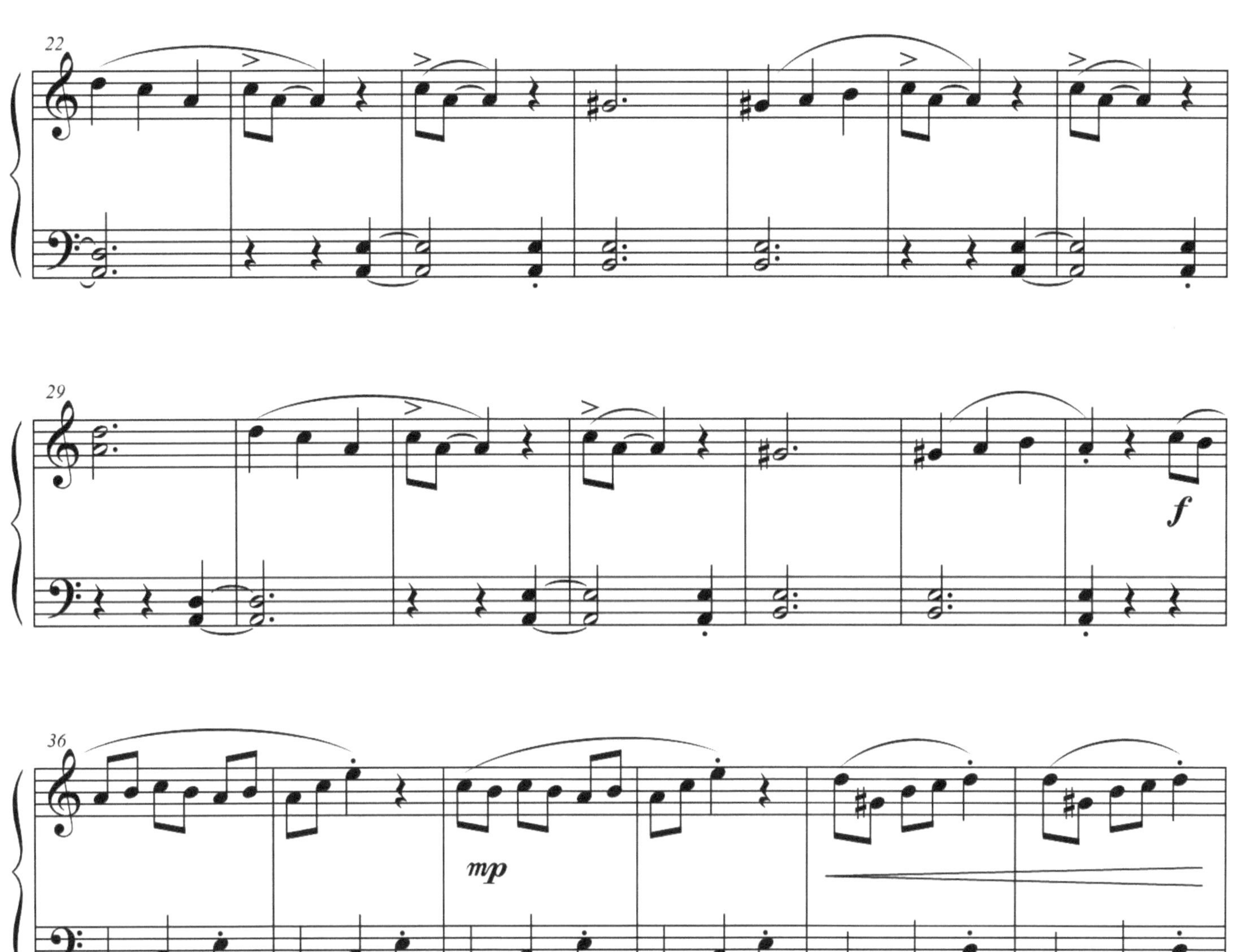
22
29
f
36
mp

WITCH'S BREW

DRAKE DESCANT

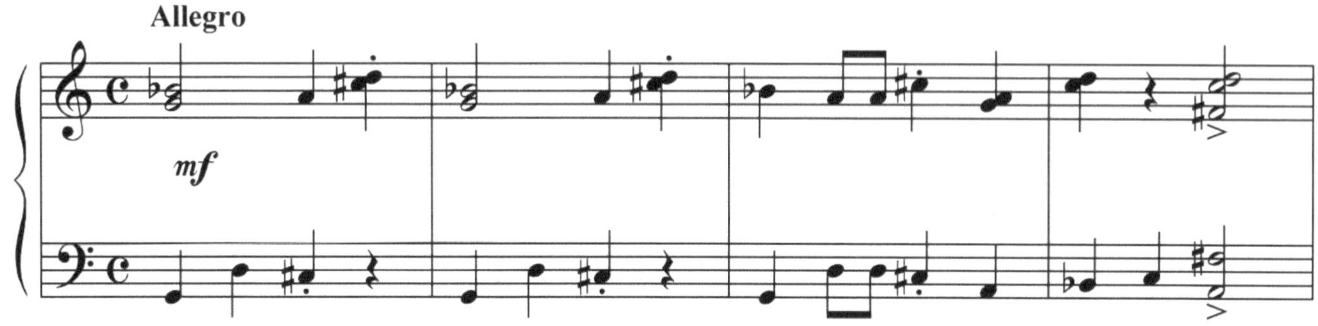

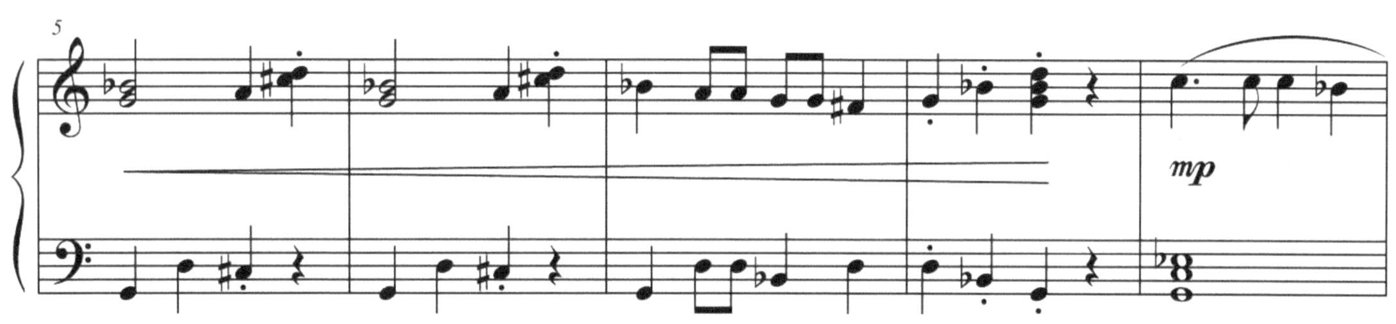

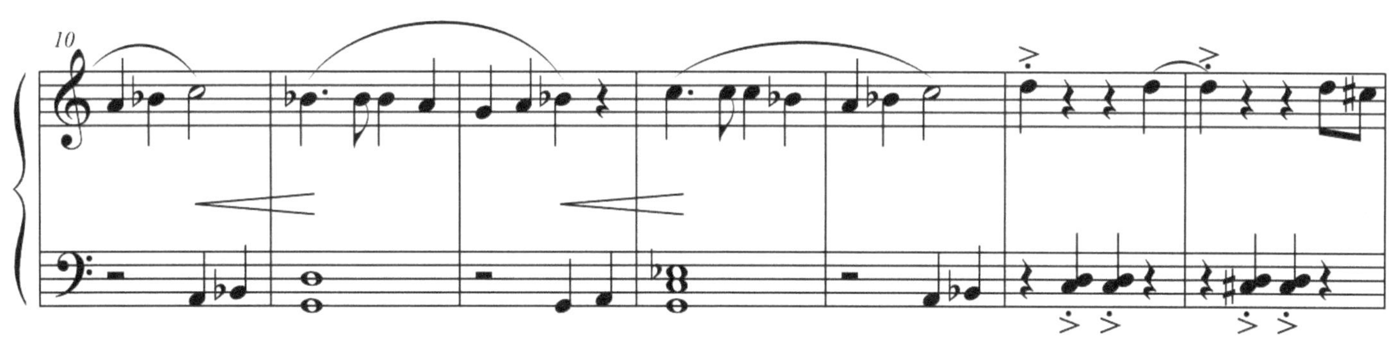

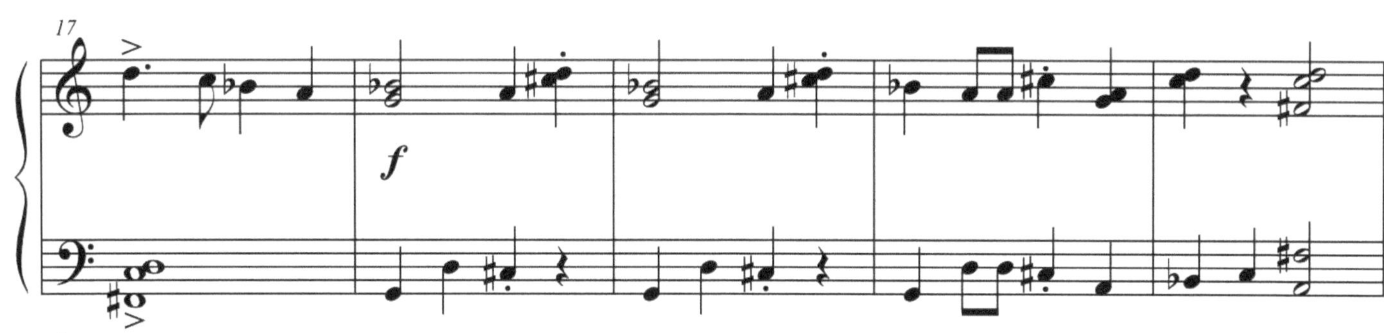

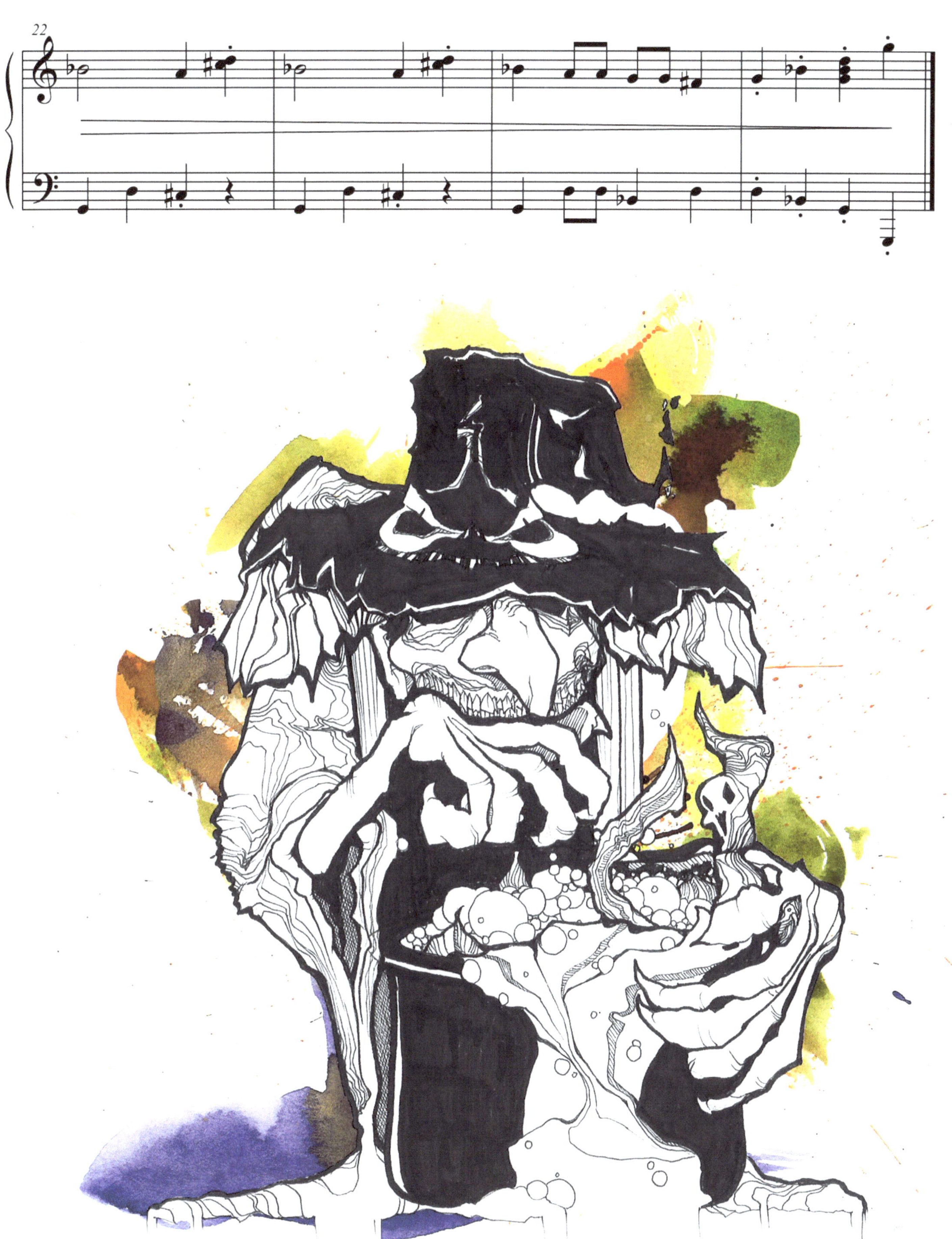
22

HAUNTED BIRTHDAY

DRAKE DESCANT

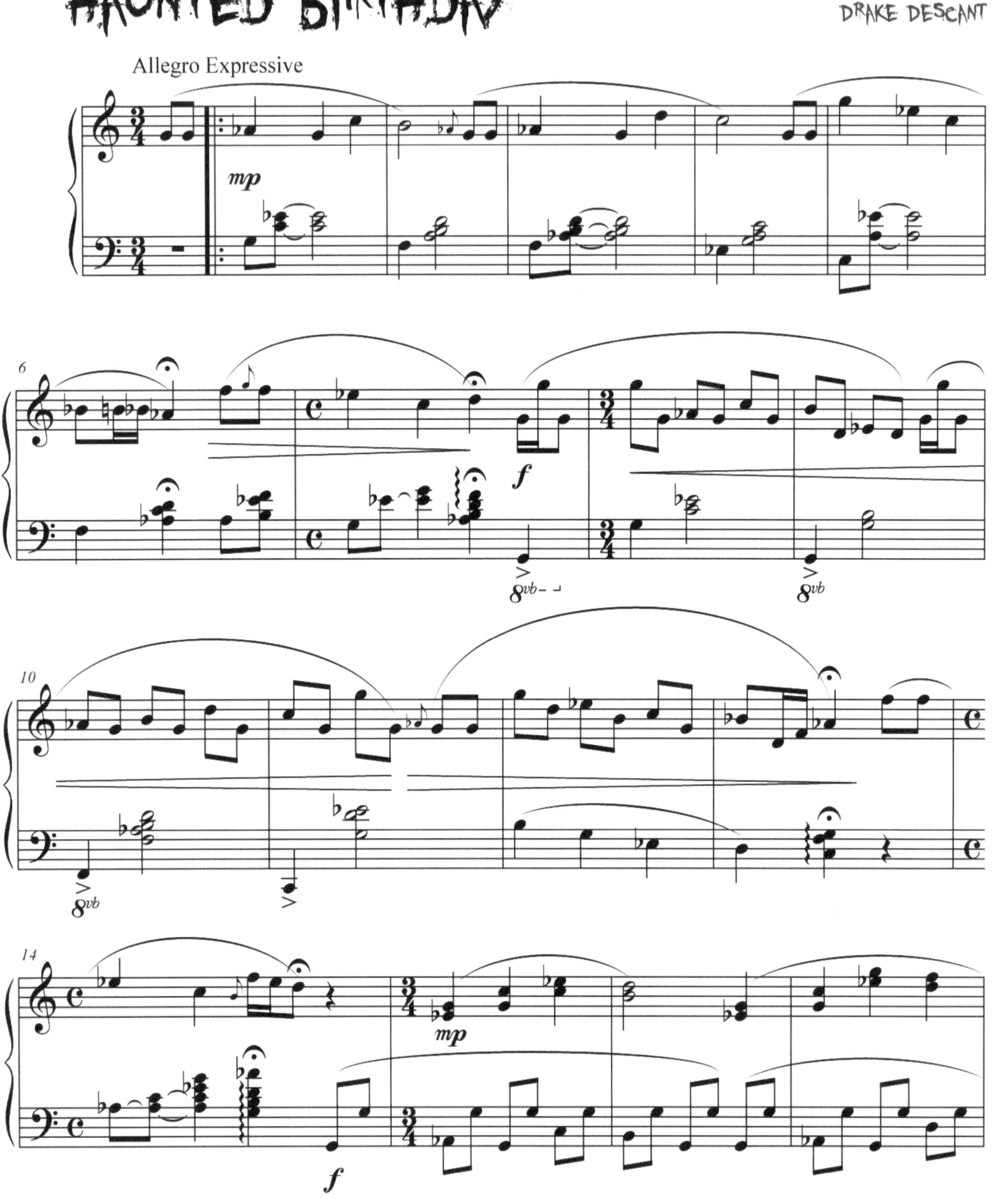

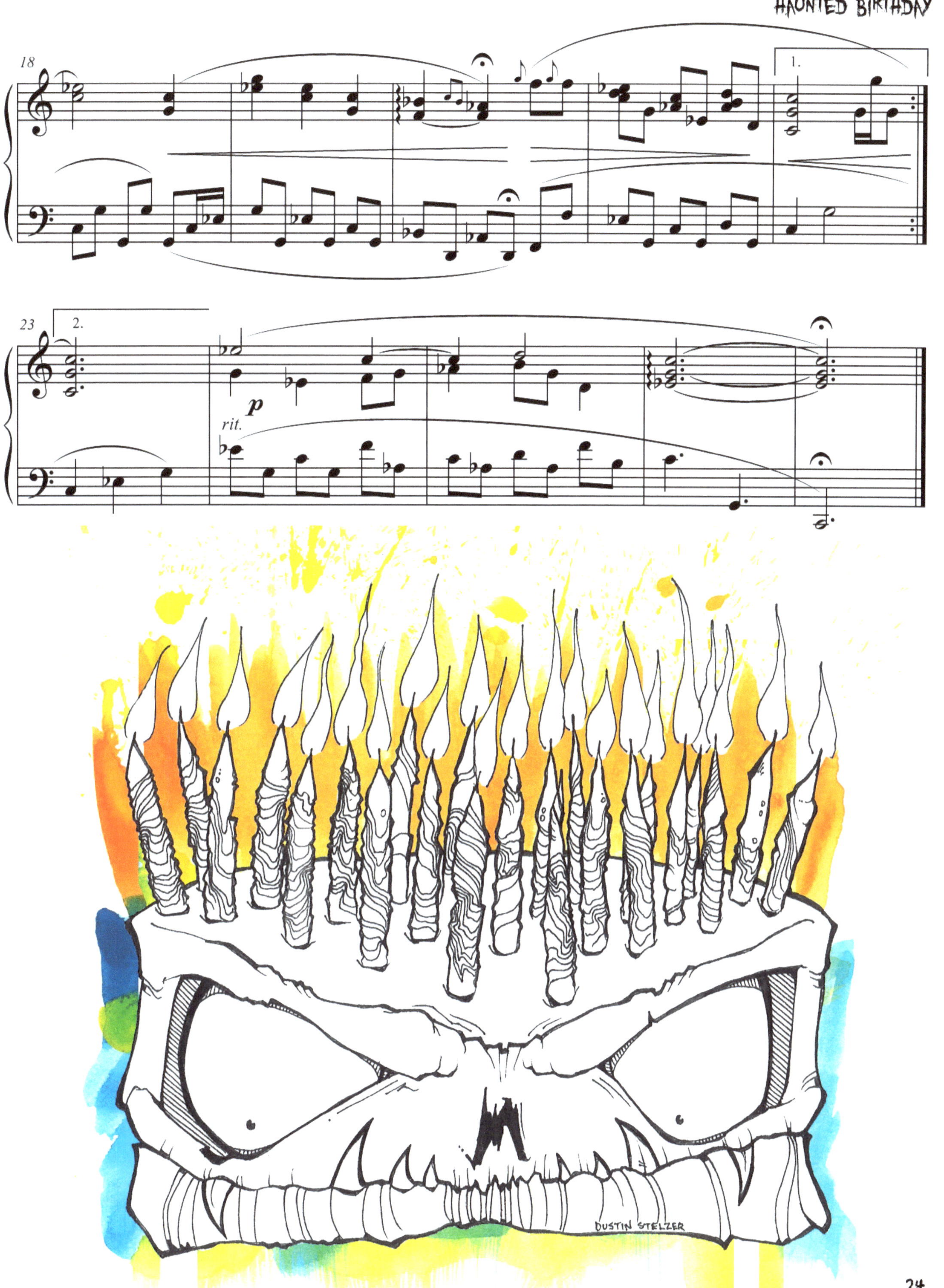
18
1.
23
2.
p
rit.
DUSTIN STELZER

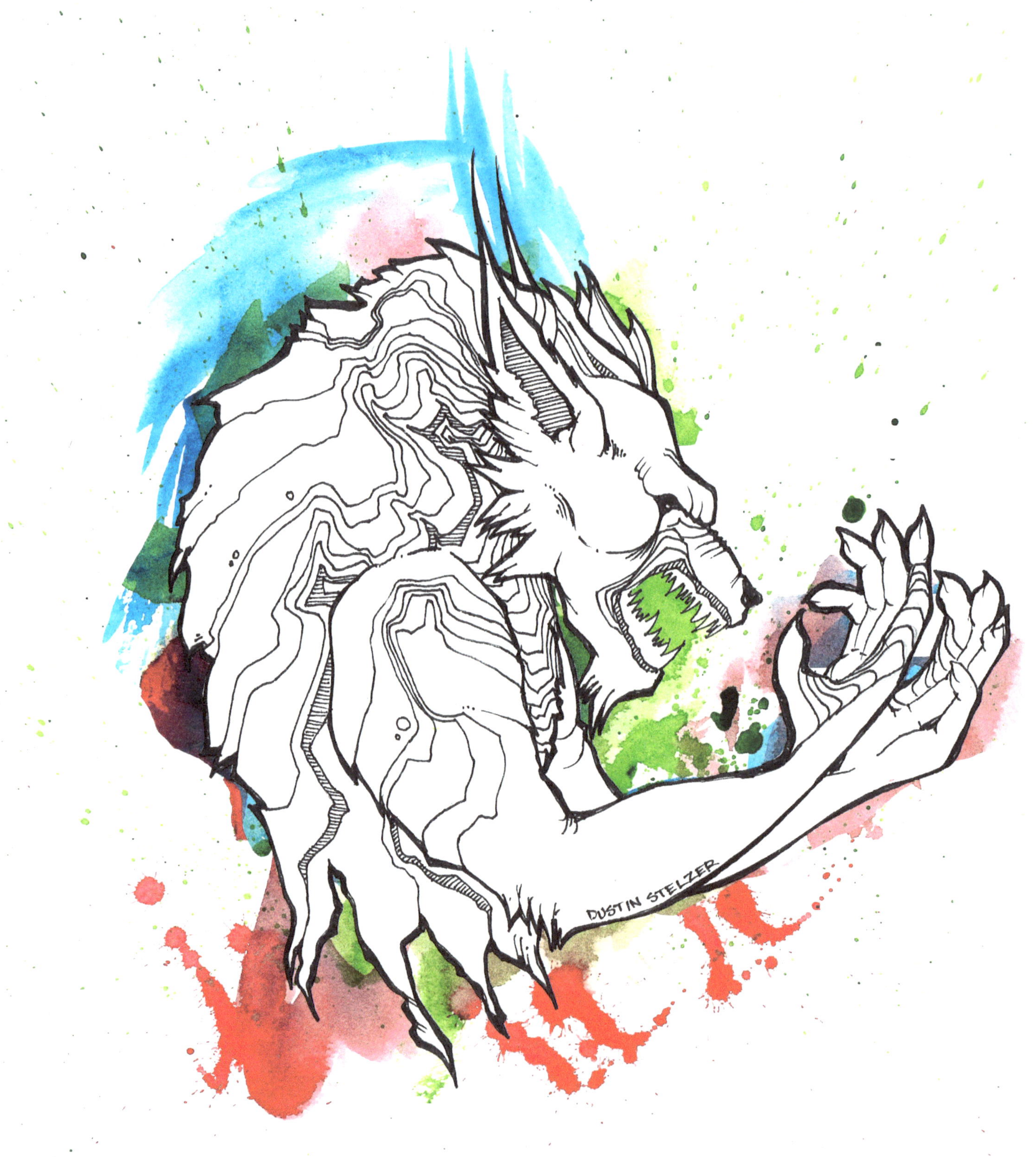
DUSTIN STELZER

The Werewolf's Awakening

Drake Descant

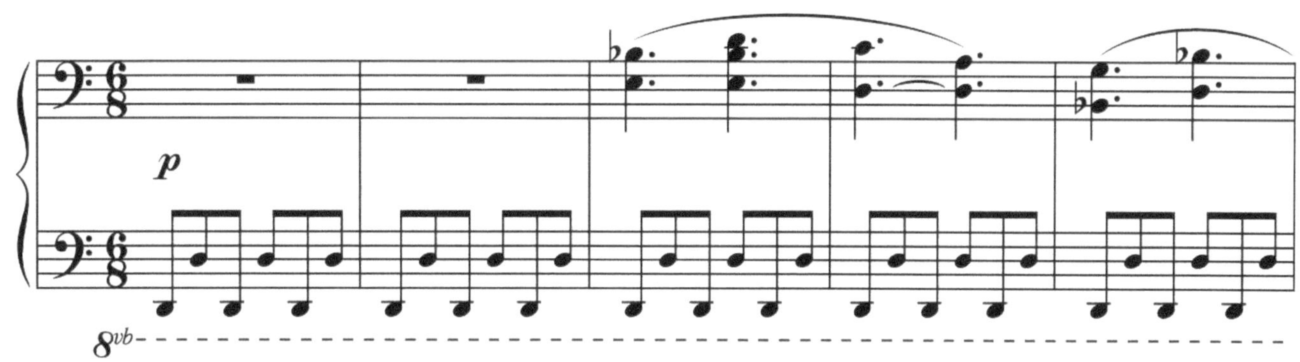

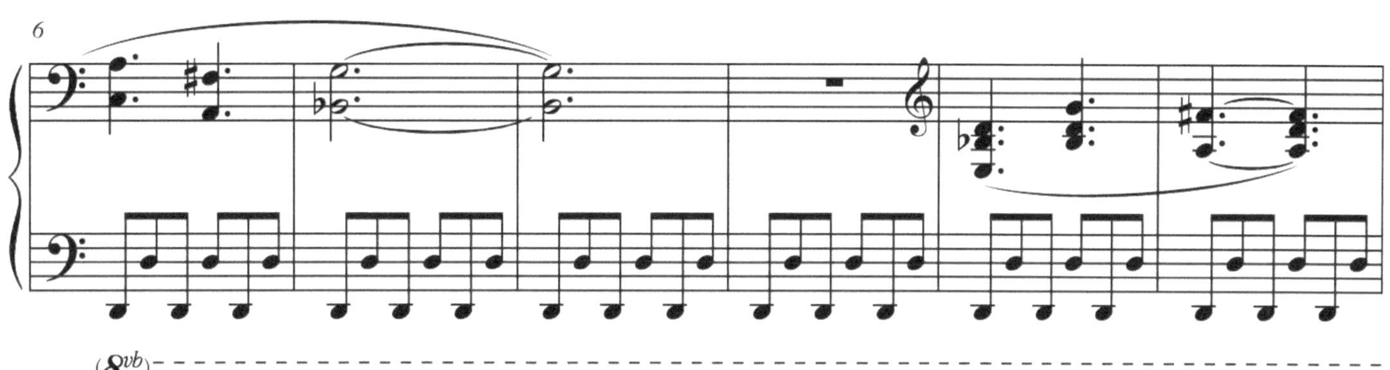

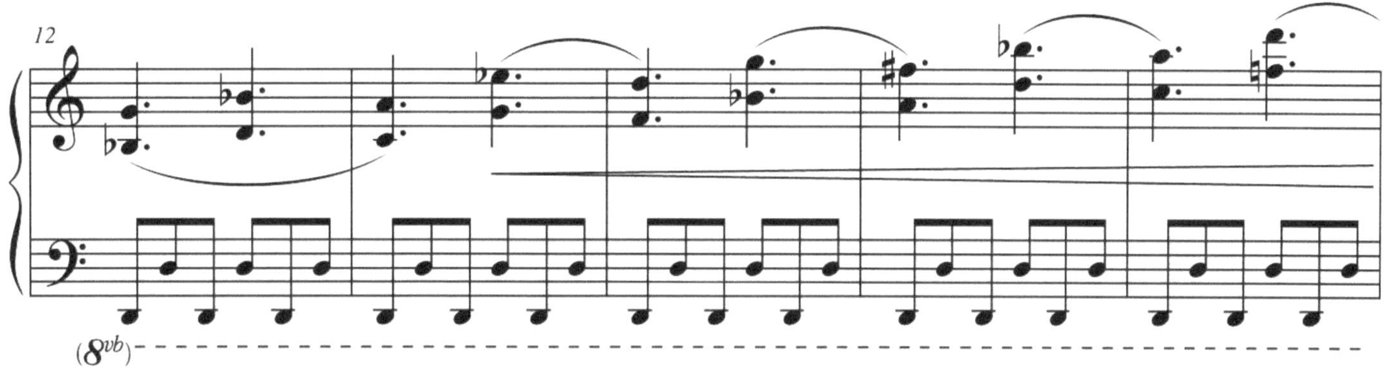

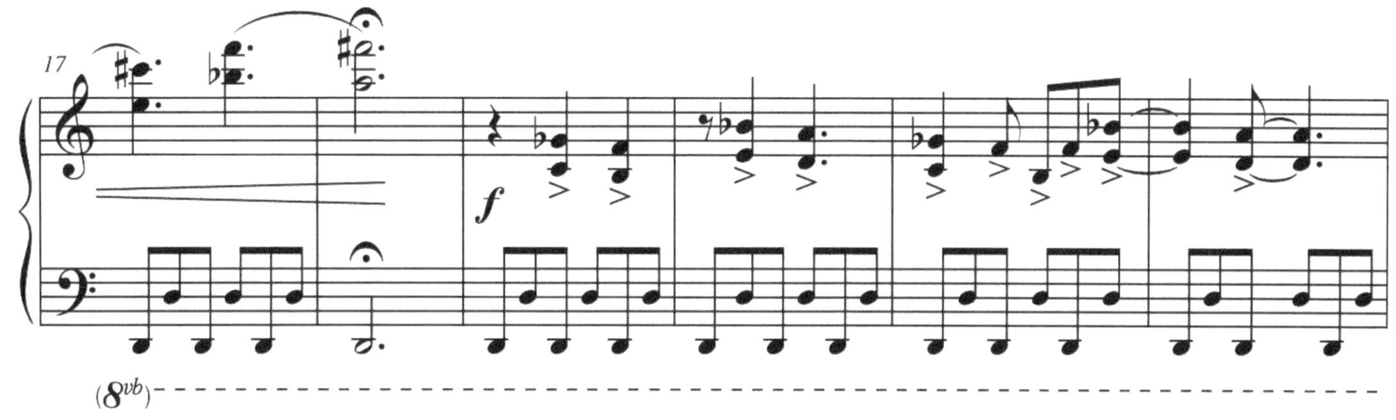

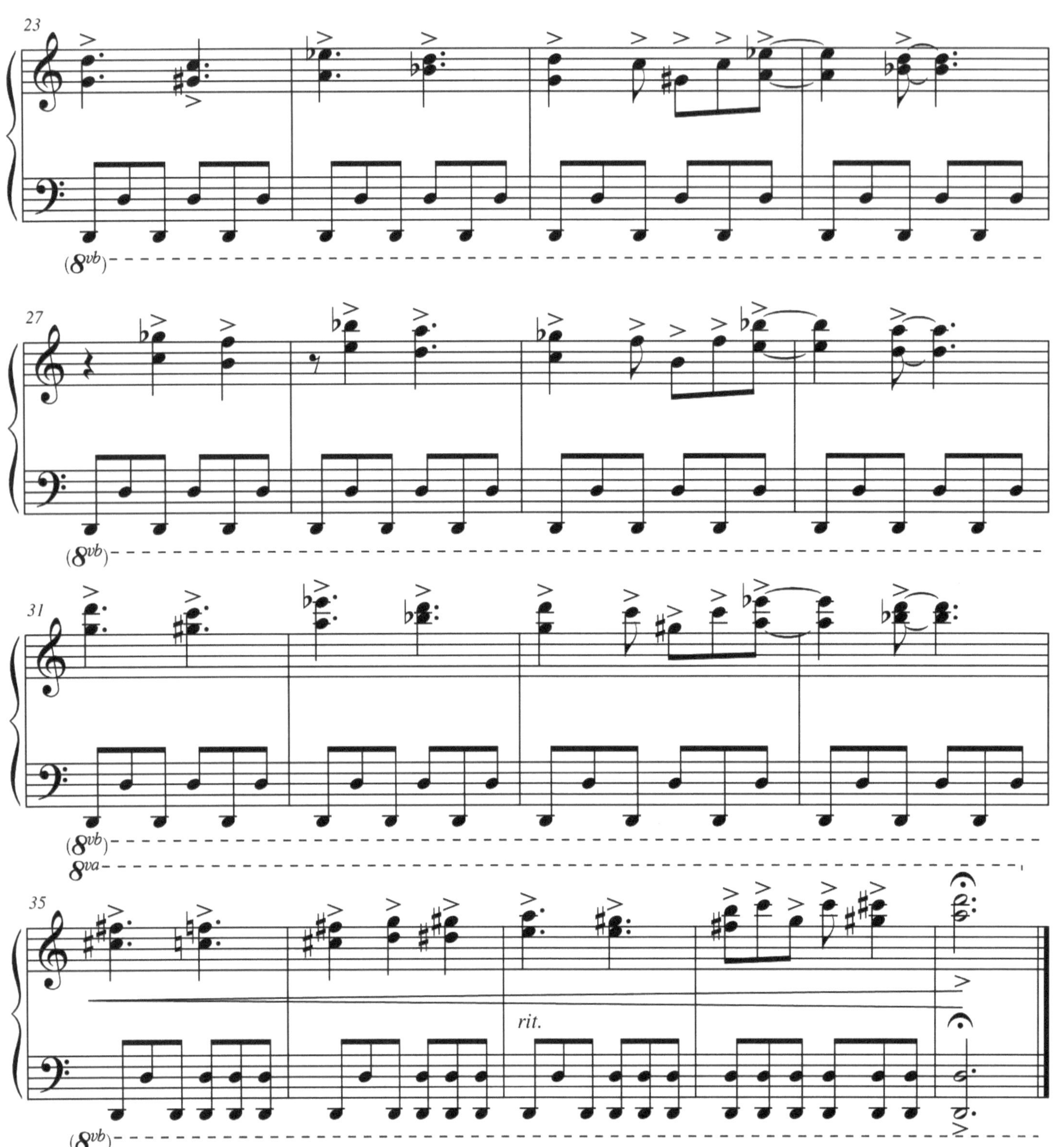
23
(8vb)
27
(8vb)
31
(8vb)
8va
35
rit.
(8vb)

www.ingramcontent.com/pod-product-compliance
Lightning Source LLC
LaVergne TN
LVHW070224110826
845147LV00003B/642
* 9 7 8 0 6 9 2 4 9 3 9 1 5 *